Lessons
on
Liberty

Brian Mecham

ISBN: 1981370803
ISBN-13: 978-1981370801

CONTENTS

INTRODUCTION

The following educational lessons have been designed to guide you through an understanding of the principles of Liberty – Agency, Freedom, God-given Rights, The Proper Role of Government, The Constitution, Free Enterprise, Secret Combinations, God's Law, and more. This information is presented from a gospel perspective and includes teachings from Ezra Taft Benson, Joseph Smith, W. Cleon Skousen and others.

THE WAR IN HEAVEN ON EARTH TODAY

"Every person on the earth today chose the right side during the war in heaven. Be on the right side now." (Ezra Taft Benson[1])

The doctrine of a war in Heaven is not exclusive to the Church of Jesus Christ of Latter-day Saints.

"And there was war in heaven: Michael and his angels fought against the dragon; and the dragon fought and his angels, And prevailed not; neither was their place found any more in heaven. And the great dragon was cast out, that old serpent, called the Devil, and Satan, which deceiveth the whole world: he was cast out into the earth, and his angels were cast out with him." (Revelation 12:7-9.)

Though all Bible believing religions recognize a war in Heaven, modern revelation has given us additional insights into what the war was all about.

"Wherefore, because that Satan rebelled against me, and sought to destroy the agency of man, which

I, the Lord God, had given him, and also, that I should give unto him mine own power; by the power of mine Only Begotten, I caused that he should be cast down..." (Moses 4:3.)

President David O McKay said:

"There are two contending Forces. Those forces are known and have been designated by different terms throughout the ages. In the beginning they were known as Satan on the one hand, and Christ on the other... In these days, they are called domination by the state, on one hand, personal liberty, on the other."[2]

President Ezra Taft Benson said:

"The central issue in the premortal council was: Shall the children of God have untrammeled agency to choose the course they should follow, whether good or evil, or shall they be coerced and forced to be obedient? Christ and all who followed him stood for the former proposition-freedom of choice; Satan stood for the latter-coercion and force. The war that began in heaven over this issue is not yet over. The conflict continues on the battlefield of mortality. And one of Lucifer's primary strategies has been to restrict our agency through the power of earthly governments."[3]

Elder Marion G. Romney said:

"Man is in the earth to be tested. The issue as to

whether he succeeds or fails will be determined by how he uses his agency. His whole future, through all eternity, is at stake. Abridge man's agency, and the whole purpose of his mortality is thwarted. Without it, the Lord says, there is no existence. The Lord so valued our agency that he designed and dictated 'the laws and constitution' required to guarantee it. This he explained in the revelation in which he instructed the Prophet Joseph Smith to appeal for help:

"According to the laws and constitution of the people, which I have suffered to be established, and should be maintained for the rights and protection of all flesh, according to just and holy principles; that every man may act in doctrine and principle pertaining to futurity, according to the moral agency which I have given unto him, that every man may be accountable for his own sins in the day of judgment. And for this purpose have I established the Constitution of this land by the hands of wise men whom I raised up unto this very purpose." (D&C 101:77-78, 80.)[4]

President John Taylor said:

"Besides the preaching of the Gospel, we have another mission, namely, the perpetuation of the free agency of man and the maintenance of liberty, freedom, and the rights of man."[5]

Reiterating the importance of the Constitution, President David O. McKay said, and more recently,

Elder L. Tom Perry repeated:

"Next to being one in worshiping God there is nothing in this world upon which this Church should be more united than in upholding and defending the Constitution of the United States."[6]

Unfortunately sometimes people look at this negatively and think this is *engaging in politics*. President Joseph F. Smith had something to say in those regards:

"There has been a tendency among some Latter-day Saints, even when the Constitution is mentioned, to say, 'There he goes talking politics.' I am not talking politics. I am quoting the words of the Lord."[7]

This is not about politics, it's about agency and freedom; it's about God's plan of salvation and the building up of His kingdom on the earth.

In what ways does Lucifer continue waging this war?

Joseph Fielding Smith said:

"Satan has control now. No matter where you look, he is in control, even in our own land. He is guiding the governments as far as the Lord will permit him. That is why there is so much strife, turmoil, confusion all over the earth. One master mind is governing the nations. It is not the

President of the United States ... it is not the king or government of England or any other land; it is Satan himself."[8]

Ezra Taft Benson said:

"Concerning the United States, the Lord revealed to his prophets that its greatest threat would be a vast, worldwide *secret combination* which would not only threaten the United States but also seek to 'overthrow the freedom of all lands, nations.'"[9]

Expounding on this, Benson said:

"Joseph Smith said that the Book of Mormon was the 'keystone of our religion' and the 'most correct' book on earth. This most correct book on earth states that the downfall of two great American civilizations came as a result of secret conspiracies whose desire was to overthrow the freedom of the people.

"Now undoubtedly Moroni could have pointed out many factors that led to the destruction of the people, but notice how he singled out the secret combinations, just as the Church today could point out many threats to peace, prosperity, and the spread of God's work, but it has singled out as the greatest threat the Godless conspiracy. There is no conspiracy theory in the Book of Mormon—it is a conspiracy fact. And along this line I would highly recommend to you a new book entitled *None Dare Call It Conspiracy.*"[10]

The scriptures describe this latter-day conspiracy that seeks to destroy the freedoms of all lands, nations and countries.

"Wherefore, O ye Gentiles, it is wisdom in God that these things should be shown unto you, that thereby ye may repent of your sins, and suffer not that these murderous combinations shall get above you, which are built up to get power and gain—and the work, yea, even the work of destruction come upon you, yea, even the sword of the justice of the Eternal God shall fall upon you, to your overthrow and destruction if ye shall suffer these things to be. Wherefore, the Lord commandeth you, when ye shall see these things come among you that ye shall awake to a sense of your awful situation, because of this secret combination which shall be among you; or wo be unto it, because of the blood of them who have been slain; for they cry from the dust for vengeance upon it, and also upon those who built it up. For it cometh to pass that whoso buildeth it up seeketh to overthrow the freedom of all lands, nations, and countries; and it bringeth to pass the destruction of all people, for it is built up by the devil, who is the father of all lies; even that same liar who beguiled our first parents, yea, even that same liar who hath caused man to commit murder from the beginning; who hath hardened the hearts of men that they have murdered the prophets, and stoned them, and cast them out from the beginning. Wherefore, I, Moroni, am commanded to write these things that evil may be done away, and that the time may come that Satan may have no power upon the hearts of the children of men, but that they may be persuaded to do good continually, that they may come unto the fountain of all righteousness and be saved." (Ether 8: 23-26.)

Ether 8:23-25, in the *Book of Mormon*, teaches us that this Latter-Day conspiracy seeks to:

- Get power
- Get gain or money
- Murder
- Overthrow freedom in all lands, nations, and countries
- Bring destruction to all people

As was shown before, the Lords prophets have admonished us to "do all we can to preserve freedom". Moroni pleads for the same here as well. He says that when we "awake to our awful situation," that we must:

- Repent of our sins
- Not allow this conspiracy to get above you

This battle is still raging on the earth today. Satan tries to trick Latter-day Saints not to "get involved" in the freedom battle.

In General Conference of April 1965, Ezra Taft Benson exposed the tactics of the evil one:

"'We really haven't received much instruction

about freedom,' the devil says. This is a lie, for we have been warned time and again. Last conference I spoke of a book embodying much of the prophets' warnings on freedom ... which I commend to you. It is entitled *Prophets, Principles, and National Survival.*

"'You're too involved in other church work,' says the devil. But freedom is a weighty matter of the law; the lesser principles of the gospel you should keep but not leave this one undone. We may have to balance and manage our time better.

"'Don't worry,' says the devil 'the Lord will protect you, and besides the world is so corrupt and heading toward destruction at such a pace that you can't stop it, so why try.' Well to begin with, the Lord will not protect us unless we do our part. But many of the prophecies referring to America's preservation are conditional. That is, if we do our duty we can be preserved, and if not then we shall be destroyed. This means that a good deal of the responsibility lies with the priesthood of this Church as to what happens to America and as to how much tragedy can be avoided if we do act now.

"'Don't do anything in the fight for freedom until the Church sets up its own specific program to save the Constitution.'

"To those slothful servants who will not do anything until they are 'compelled in all things.' Maybe the Lord will never set up a specific church program for the purpose of saving the Constitution.

"The Prophet Joseph Smith declared it will be the elders of Israel who will step forward to help save the Constitution, not the Church."[11]

"'There is no need to get involved in the fight for freedom – all you need to do is live the gospel.' Of course this is a contradiction, because we cannot fully live the gospel and not be involved in the fight for freedom."[12]

Now that we understand there are no good excuses and we need to be actively engaged, what are we to do?

In General Conference, October 1987, President Ezra Taft Benson laid out these steps:

1. *We must be righteous and moral. We must live the gospel principles – all of them.*
2. *We must learn the principles of the Constitution and then abide by its precepts.*
3. *We must become involved in civic affairs. As citizens of this republic, we cannot do our duty and be idle spectators.*
4. *We must make our influence felt by our vote, our letters, and our advice. We must be wisely informed and let others know how we feel.*

Beyond this counsel it would also be wise to seek out the guidance of the Lord. We are counseled to "search, ponder, and pray" over the scriptures to understand the truth. You are either on the discovery path or have already "searched" and have (as Moroni termed it) *awakened to our awful situation.* I recommend that you ponder these things, consider what you have learned. Take your questions to the Lord, regarding what you should do about these things, and seek to discover His will for you. Often it is after we have done our part in searching for truth and information that we receive revelation and inspiration. We each have different skills, expertise, knowledge and abilities and can be effective in different ways. Some people will create blogs, websites, videos, some will organize meetings and/or teach classes. Some people might be inspired to run for office, become a delegate, and so on. There are many possibilities. The correct answer for one person may be different for another. It's up to each of us to discover what the Lord has called us to do, and what role to play in furthering His kingdom on earth.

Elder Shirley D. Christensen emphasized this as well when he said:

"What a sacred privilege and responsibility is ours to participate with other like-minded people to ensure that basic freedoms are preserved wherever we reside."[13]

President Gordon B. Hinckley said:

"That war, so bitter, so intense, has never ceased.

It is the war... between agency and compulsion, between the followers of Christ and those who have denied Him. His enemies have used every stratagem in that conflict. They've indulged in lying and deceit. They've employed money and wealth. They've tricked the minds of men. They've murdered and destroyed and engaged in every kind of evil practice to thwart the work of Christ."[14]

It is apparent that in Satan's attempt to destroy man's freedom and agency, and thwart God's plan, he has established much control and influence over many institutions. Even the *Word of Wisdom*, which is a guide for healthy living, states that it was revelation from the Lord given "in consequence of evils and designs which do and will exist in the hearts of conspiring men in the last days" (D&C 89:4). Below is a list of just some of the realms that Satan has influence over:

- Religion / Spirituality
- Politics / Government
- Business / Economics
- Education
- Science
- Health (food and drug)
- Media / Entertainment
- News
- and more...

Elder James E. Faust said, "It is important to 'study evil, and its consequences.' Since Satan is the author of all the evil in the world, it is essential therefore to realize that he is the influence behind the opposition to the work of God. Alma stated the issue succinctly: 'Whatsoever is good cometh from God, and whatsoever is evil cometh from the devil.' (Alma 5:40.)"[15]

By understanding Satan's influence we are better armed in our search for truth in all realms of life.

In the end, the Lord wins!

President Ezra Taft Benson testified:

"The Lord has declared that before the second coming of Christ it will be necessary to 'destroy the secret works of darkness' in order to preserve the land of Zion, the Americas (2 Nephi 10:11-16)."[16]

Every person on the earth today chose the right side during the war in heaven. Be on the right side now. Stand up and be counted.

# # #

Recommended Resources:

- Video: *The War In Heaven Continues On Earth Today.* YouTube, ldsconservative channel

- Book: *Stand Up For Freedom*, Ezra Taft Benson. Available at ldsfreedombooks.com or amazon.com

LIFE, LIBERTY AND THE PURSUIT OF HAPPINESS

God is the source of all light, truth and intelligence. He is also the source of Man's rights.

From the *Declaration of Independence*:

"We hold these truths to be self-evident, that all men are created equal, that they are endowed by their Creator with certain unalienable Rights, that among these are Life, Liberty and the pursuit of Happiness."

The *Declaration of Independence* asserted that God has given us certain fundamental rights. These are rights that are not to be violated by anyone, not even government. We may forfeit some of these rights, and face certain consequences, if we choose to infringe upon the rights of others.

In his speech on the *Proper Role of Government*, Ezra Taft Benson said the following:

"The great Thomas Jefferson asked: 'Can the liberties of a nation be thought secure when we have removed their only firm basis, a conviction in the minds of the people that these liberties are of the gift of God? That they are not to be violated but with his wrath?'

"Starting at the foundation of the pyramid, let us first consider the origin of those freedoms we have come to know are human rights. There are only two possible sources. Rights are either God-given as part of the Divine Plan, or they are granted by government as part of the political plan. Reason, necessity, tradition and religious convictions all lead me to accept the divine origin of these rights. If we accept the premise that human rights are granted by government, then we must be willing to accept the corollary that they can be denied by government. I, for one, shall never accept that premise. As the French political economist, Frédéric Bastiat, phrased it so succinctly, 'Life, liberty, and property do not exist because men have made laws. On the contrary, it was the fact that life, liberty, and property existed beforehand that caused men to make laws in the first place.' (The Law)."[1]

Consider the following statement by David O. McKay:

"If man is to be rewarded for righteousness and punished for evil, then common justice demands that he be given the power of independent action. ... If he were coerced to do right at all times, or were

14

helplessly enticed to commit sin, he would merit neither a blessing for the first nor punishment for the second."3

What is a Fundamental Right?

Fundamental rights are those rights which all people can simultaneously claim without forcing someone to serve their needs.

With this definition in mind it becomes much easier to determine what is a right and what is not. For example, healthcare is not actually a right, beyond you having the right to take care of your own health. You cannot force a doctor to provide services to you without violating that doctor's rights. Another example would be public education. Some believe they have a right to public education but it comes at the expense of forcing your neighbors to pay for your education, to pay for buildings, teachers, etc. What you do have the right to is educating yourself.

What is the difference between Agency, Freedom and Liberty?

Let us consider the scriptures which use these three terms in a way that implies separate meanings:

"Wherefore, men are **free** according to the flesh; and all things are given them which are expedient unto man. And they are **free to choose liberty** and eternal life, through the great Mediator of all men, or to choose captivity and death, according to the captivity and power of the devil; for he seeketh that all men might be miserable like unto himself." (2 Nephi 2:27.)

Analyze the statement "they are free to choose liberty". *You may also want to read the surrounding verses in that chapter to get the full context.*

We are told that we are *free to choose liberty or captivity.* The choice implies that we have agency, or the ability to choose between different paths, and also that we have the freedom to act on those choices.

Agency is the ability to choose an action, whereas freedom is the capability to do an action. What's the difference? Here's an example: A prisoner in solitary confinement could sincerely make the decision to be kind to everyone. They could make that choice, despite not being able to actually interact with anyone. While they lack the freedom, or capability, to actually show kindness to others, there is nothing preventing them from being the type of person that would act that way given the opportunity to do so. Agency is the ability to choose an action, whereas freedom is the capability to actually do the action.

Liberty is presented as being opposite of captivity. Liberty is often confused as having the same meaning as freedom, yet there is a difference. I've defined freedom as the capability of acting on your choices. Liberty comes from choosing and doing righteous actions, those which are just before God. It's really impossible to separate liberty from obedience to the laws of God.

Real liberty comes from obeying a commandment or law to reach the destination you want. Captivity is choosing a path and being bound to the outcome, whereas liberty is choosing your destination or outcome and being bound to the path required to achieve such an outcome.

The key to understanding and experiencing liberty lies in choosing the outcome we want versus receiving the outcome our path dictates.

If you want the liberty that comes from being healthy and having the ability to *run an not be weary, walk and not faint* (see D&C 89), you must choose that outcome of healthiness and have your path dictated accordingly. If you are committed to that outcome you are not going to consume sugary treats and soda pop all day – that choice would bind you to the outcome inherent in unhealthy living, and you would be in bondage.

We can "choose liberty and eternal life, through the great Mediator of all men, or choose captivity and death, according to the captivity and power of the devil". It is only through choosing the plan of God, through Christ and His plan of salvation that we can truly have and experience liberty. This was also the understanding of America's founding fathers. "Our constitution," said John Adams, "was made only for a moral and religious people. It is wholly inadequate to the government of any other".

Going back to 2nd Nephi Chapter 2, verse 25, we read that "men are that they might have joy". It is in choosing liberty that we will experience lasting joy or happiness.

To choose liberty is to choose to stand up for truth and righteousness, to be found on the Lord's side. Choosing liberty results in experiencing the ultimate level of freedom.

This gives a new meaning to the words "life, liberty and happiness". This life is a time for us to be "tried, to be tested, and to choose. Our decisions determine our destiny... Those who choose the Lord's way" (choose liberty) and "who prove faithful shall inherit the kingdom of God, ... and their joy shall be full forever."[3]

"And ye shall know the truth, and the truth shall make you free." (John 8:32.)

"Where the Spirit of the Lord is, there is liberty." (2 Corinthians 3: 17.)

# # #

Recommended Resources:

- Video: *What is a Fundamental Right?*. YouTube, ldsconservative channel

- Video: *Moral Agency & Natural Law*. YouTube, ldsconservative channel

- Video: *Natural Law: The Moral Basis of a Free Society* by Stephen Pratt. YouTube, ldsconservative channel

THE PROPER ROLE OF GOVERNMENT

An understanding of the proper role of government is essential and one of the most important principles for a free people. Without an adequate and correct understanding of your God-given fundamental rights, and an understanding of the proper role of government in relation to those rights, we cannot make informed and educated choices in the selection of leaders to serve as our representatives in government. Our choices in this regard have eternal consequences and can negatively affect hundreds, or even millions, of people.

H. Verlan Andersen commented on agency saying:

"Not only does your every political decision involve the free agency of others, but that of numerous people."[1]

Quoting from *The Law* by Frédéric Bastiat:

"Existence, faculties, assimilation — in other words, personality, liberty, property — this is man.

"It is of these three things that it may be said, apart from all demagogue subtlety, that they are anterior and superior to all human legislation.

"**It is not because men have made laws, that personality, liberty, and property exist. On the contrary, it is because personality, liberty, and property exist beforehand, that men make laws**. What, then, is law? As I have said elsewhere, it is the collective organization of the individual right to lawful defense.

"Nature, or rather God, has bestowed upon every one of us the right to defend his person, his liberty, and his property, since these are the three constituent or preserving elements of life; elements, each of which is rendered complete by the others, and cannot be understood without them. For what are our faculties, but the extension of our personality? and what is property, but an extension of our faculties?

"If every man has the right of defending, even by force, his person, his liberty, and his property, a number of men have the right to combine together, to extend, to organize a common force, to provide regularly for this defense.

"Collective right, then, has its principle, its reason for existing, its lawfulness, in individual right; and the common force cannot rationally have any other end, or any other mission, than that of the isolated forces for which it is substituted. Thus, as the force of an individual cannot lawfully touch the person, the liberty, or the property of another individual — for the same reason, the common force cannot lawfully be used to destroy the person, the liberty, or the property of individuals or of classes.

"For this perversion of force would be, in one case as in the other, in contradiction to our premises. For who will dare to say that force has been given to us, not to defend our rights, but to annihilate the equal rights of our brethren? And if this be not true of every individual force, acting independently, how can it be true of the collective force, which is only the organized union of isolated forces?

"Nothing, therefore, can be more evident than this: The law is the organization of the natural right of lawful defense; it is the substitution of collective for individual forces, for the purpose of acting in the sphere in which they have a right to act, of doing what they have a right to do, to secure persons, liberties, and properties, and to maintain each in its right, so as to cause justice to reign over all."[2]

Excerpts from Ezra Taft Benson's *Proper Role of Government*:

"Unlike the political opportunist, the true statesman values principle above popularity, and works to create popularity for those political principles which are wise and just.

"It is generally agreed that the most important single function of government is to secure the rights and freedoms of individual citizens. But, what are those right? And what is their source? Until these questions are answered there is little likelihood that we can correctly determine how government can best secure them.

"The proper function of government is limited only to those spheres of activity within which the individual citizen has the right to act. By deriving its just powers from the governed, government becomes primarily a mechanism for defense against bodily harm, theft and involuntary servitude. It cannot claim the power to redistribute the wealth or force reluctant citizens to perform acts of charity against their will. Government is created by man. No man possesses such power to delegate. The creature cannot exceed the creator.

"In general terms, therefore, the proper role of government includes such defensive activities, as maintaining national military and local police forces for protection against loss of life, loss of property, and loss of liberty at the hands of either foreign despots or domestic criminals."3

The Proper Role of Government, by Ezra Taft Benson, is essential reading material and is freely available to listen, watch, or read online at properroleofgovernment.com.

Quoting again from *The Proper Role of Government*:

"As a conclusion to this discussion, I present a declaration of principles which have recently been prepared by a few American patriots, and to which I wholeheartedly subscribe.

Fifteen Principles Which Make For Good And Proper Government

"As an Independent American for constitutional government I declare that:

1. I believe that no people can maintain freedom unless their political institutions are founded upon faith in God and belief in the existence of moral law.

2. I believe that God has endowed men with certain unalienable rights as set forth in the Declaration of Independence and that no legislature and no majority, however great, may morally limit or destroy these; that the sole function of government is to protect life, liberty, and property and anything more than this is usurpation and oppression.

3. I believe that the Constitution of the United States was prepared and adopted by men acting under inspiration from Almighty God;

that it is a solemn compact between the peoples of the States of this nation which all officers of government are under duty to obey; that the eternal moral laws expressed therein must be adhered to or individual liberty will perish.

4. I believe it a violation of the Constitution for government to deprive the individual of either life, liberty, or property except for these purposes: (a) Punish crime and provide for the administration of justice; (b) Protect the right and control of private property; (c) Wage defensive war and provide for the nation's defense; (d) Compel each one who enjoys the protection of government to bear his fair share of the burden of performing the above functions.

5. I hold that the Constitution denies government the power to take from the individual either his life, liberty, or property except in accordance with moral law; that the same moral law which governs the actions of men when acting alone is also applicable when they act in concert with others; that no citizen or group of citizens has any right to direct their agent, the government to perform any act which would be evil or offensive to the conscience if that citizen were performing the act himself outside the framework of government.

6. I am hereby resolved that under no circumstances shall the freedoms guaranteed by the Bill of Rights be infringed. In particular I am opposed to any attempt on the part of the Federal Government to deny the people their right to bear arms, to worship and pray when and where they choose, or to own and control private property.

7. I consider ourselves at war with international Communism which is committed to the destruction of our government, our right of property, and our freedom; that it is treason as defined by the Constitution to give aid and comfort to this implacable enemy.

8. I am unalterable opposed to Socialism, either in whole or in part, and regard it as an unconstitutional usurpation of power and a denial of the right of private property for government to own or operate the means of producing and distributing goods and services in competition with private enterprise, or to regiment owners in the legitimate use of private property.

9. I maintain that every person who enjoys the protection of his life, liberty, and property should bear his fair share of the cost of government in providing that protection; that the elementary principles of justice set forth in the Constitution demand that all taxes imposed be uniform and that each person's

property or income be taxed at the same rate.

10. I believe in honest money, the gold and silver coinage of the Constitution, and a circulation medium convertible into such money without loss. I regard it as a flagrant violation of the explicit provisions of the Constitution for the Federal Government to make it a criminal offense to use gold or silver coin as legal tender or to use irredeemable paper money.

11. I believe that each State is sovereign in performing those functions reserved to it by the Constitution and it is destructive of our federal system and the right of self-government guaranteed under the Constitution for the Federal Government to regulate or control the States in performing their functions or to engage in performing such functions itself.

12. I consider it a violation of the Constitution for the Federal Government to levy taxes for the support of state or local government; that no State or local government can accept funds from the Federal and remain independent in performing its functions, nor can the citizens exercise their rights of self-government under such conditions.

13. I deem it a violation of the right of private property guaranteed under the Constitution for the Federal Government to forcibly

deprive the citizens of this nation of their nation of their property through taxation or otherwise, and make a gift thereof to foreign governments or their citizens.

14. I believe that no treaty or agreement with other countries should deprive our citizens of rights guaranteed them by the Constitution.

15. I consider it a direct violation of the obligation imposed upon it by the Constitution for the Federal Government to dismantle or weaken our military establishment below that point required for the protection of the States against invasion, or to surrender or commit our men, arms, or money to the control of foreign ore world organizations of governments. These things I believe to be the proper role of government.

"We have strayed far afield. We must return to basic concepts and principles – to eternal verities. There is no other way. The storm signals are up. They are clear and ominous."

The scriptures also contain statements regarding the role of government. From *Doctrine & Covenants* section 134:

"We believe that governments were instituted of God for the benefit of man; and that he holds men accountable for their acts in relation to them, both in making laws and administering them, for the good and safety of society.

"We believe that no government can exist in peace, except such laws are framed and held inviolate as will secure to each individual the free exercise of conscience, the right and control of property, and the protection of life..."

These principles on the role of government, expressed by Ezra Taft Benson, Frédéric Bastiat, and others, are just as essential and valid today as they were when the words were written/spoken.

# # #

Recommended Resources:

- Article: *The Proper Role of Government* by Ezra Taft Benson. Visit: properroleofgovernment.com

- Video: *The Proper Role of Government* by Ezra Taft Benson. YouTube, ldsconservative channel

- Video: *Man, Freedom, Government* by Ezra Taft Benson. YouTube, ldsconservative channel

- Video: *The Standard of Good Government* by Stephen Pratt. YouTube, ldsconservative channel

- Book: *The Law* by Frédéric Bastiat. Available online

OVERVIEW OF AMERICA

In this lesson we will review some aspects of America that made it great, its inspired founding, as well as some of the troubles we face as a nation today. Unfortunately today America, as a people, has allowed themselves to become complacent and ignorant and have adopted many principles that are anti-liberty and opposite of God's Law and the principles of righteousness. In our cities, states and national government the majority of the people are voting for corrupt leaders instead of liberty-minded statesmen. Let us be reminded of what is required for America, or any nation, to remain free.

Ezra Taft Benson said:

"To us, this is not just another nation not just a member of the family of nations. This is a great and glorious nation with a divine mission and a prophetic history and future. It has been brought into being under the inspiration of heaven.

"It is our firm belief, as Latter-day Saints, that the Constitution of this land was established by men whom the God of heaven raised up unto that very purpose. It is our conviction also that the God of heaven guided the founding fathers in establishing it for his particular purpose.

"The founders of this republic were deeply spiritual men. They believed men are capable of self-government and that it is the job of government to protect freedom and foster private initiative.

"Our earliest American fathers came here with a common objective–freedom of worship and liberty of conscience. Familiar with the sacred scriptures, they believed that liberty is a gift of heaven. To them, man as a child of God emphasized the sacredness of the individual and the interest of a kind Providence in the affairs of men and nations. These leaders recognized the need for divine guidance and the importance of vital religion and morality in the affairs of men and nations.

"To the peoples who should inhabit this blessed land of the Americas, the Western Hemisphere, an ancient prophet uttered this significant promise and solemn warning: "Behold, this is a choice land, and whatsoever nation shall possess it shall be free from bondage, and from captivity, and from all other nations under heaven if they will but serve the God of the land, who is Jesus Christ, . . .

'For behold, this is a land which is choice above all other lands, wherefore he that doth possess it shall serve God or shall be swept off; for it is the everlasting decree of God....' (Ether 2:12, 10.)

"The establishment of this great Christian nation, with a spiritual foundation, was all in preparation for the restoration of the gospel, following the long night of apostasy. Then in 1820 the time had arrived. God the Father and his Son Jesus Christ made their glorious appearance. I give you a few words from the Prophet Joseph Smith, who was the instrument in God's hands in restoring the gospel and establishing the true Church of Christ again upon the earth."[1]

Again from Ezra Taft Benson:

"We should pay no attention to the recommendations of men who call the Constitution an eighteenth-century agrarian document — who apologize for capitalism and free enterprise. We should refuse to follow their siren song of concentrating, increasingly, the powers of government in the Chief Executive, of delegating American sovereign authority to non-American institutions in the United Nations, and pretending that it will bring peace to the world by turning our armed forces over to a U.N. world-wide police force.[2]

"Our Founding Fathers, with solemn and reverent expression, voiced their allegiance to the sovereignty of God, knowing that they were accountable to Him in the day of judgment. Are we less accountable today? I think not. I urge you to keep the commandments and to pray for our nation and its leaders."3

No doubt America has been blessed with many years of freedom, in comparison to other nations in the history of this world, but that freedom can only last as long as the people are moral and righteous.

W. Cleon Skousen wrote about what he called the *100 Things Destroying America*:

"The average citizen finds his orderly world eroding or even crumbling beneath his feet. His savings have recently become a very slippery kind of security. Taxes, inflation, and high interest rates are ravenously gnawing away at his dwindling standard of living. His hopes of a pleasant and safe retirement are proving illusionary. He has a feeling that he is being propagandized. programmed and over-governed to the point where his personal freedom seems to be shrinking on all fronts.

"Who has been tampering with the soul of America? We are all of us responsible. If Washington has been making us more socialist, it's because we, as citizens, have been asking Washington to do so."4

Skousen suggested that some of the things destroying America include: A deteriorating money system, a rapidly national debt, policy of deficit spending, overwhelming burden of stifling taxation, the strangulation of the free-enterprise system with over-regulation and over-taxation, a highly discriminatory welfare program now on the verge of bankruptcy, billions in foreign aid, corporate bail outs, and many more issues which he puts into multiple classifications.

- Unconstitutional Expenditure of Federal Funds
- Unconstitutional Expansion of Presidential Powers
- Unconstitutional Expansion of Judicial Power
- Unconstitutional Withholding of Land From the States
- Forces Wrecking World Stability and Fostering Predatory War
- Impact of Many Supreme Court Cases on the Security of the United States
- Unconstitutional Regulatory Agencies

Skousen also suggests a remedy for the problems facing America:

"The remedy requires that Americans rediscover the genius of the founders' original success formula and then elect the kind of men and women who will restore the formula. This can happen the moment the majority of the men and women in Congress realize that the original Constitutional and a free-market economy are the only way to go.

"Part of the remedy could be adopted immediately, part of it set up on a long-range basis. Stabilizing the dollar with precious metal backing and deregulating business should be undertaken immediately. Then the phasing out of unconstitutional programs could follow just as soon as the private sector is able to begin absorbing the two or three million people who will be coming off the Federal and State payrolls."5

In his talk entitled *America at the Crossroads*, Ezra Taft Benson suggested five things we can do to actually *make America great again* (this would also apply to other nations):

"I wonder if we in America are rearing a generation that seemingly does not understand the fundamentals of God's commandments or the principles upon which our country was founded. These principles are the secret to America's greatness! The central issue before the people today is the same issue that inflamed the hearts of our Founding Father patriots in 1776 to strike out for independence. That issue is whether the individual exists for the state or whether the state exists for the individual.

"Now you ask what you can do as one individual or family to influence your community and thereby contribute to a cure of the ailments that afflict our body politic today? I know of no better question a citizen could ask himself than that. May I suggest a few things which I believe would be beneficial.

"1. May I urge you to keep your own families strong. A nation is no stronger than the sum total of its families. If you accept the truth of that statement, then you must conclude that the American family has serious problems... The answer is for both [the father and the mother] to teach their children fundamental spiritual principles that will instill faith in God, faith in one's country, and faith in one's family.

"2. I would respectfully urge you to live by the fundamental principles of work, thrift, and self-reliance and to teach your children by your example. It was never intended in God's divine plan that man should live off the labor of someone else. Live within your own earnings. Put a portion of those earnings regularly into savings. Avoid unnecessary debt... You can ask God's blessings and his protecting care on you and your family. You are contributing to the solution of our country's ills, rather than contributing to its problems.

"3. May I humbly urge you to learn about the Constitution, the Declaration of Independence, and other basic documents of our great country so that you can sustain it and the free institutions set up under it. It is a part of my faith that the Constitution of the United States was inspired by God. I reverence it akin to the revelations that have come from God. The Lord declared he established it "by the hands of wise men whom [he] raised up unto this very purpose." (D&C 101:80.) Referring to the principles thereof, the Prophet Joseph Smith, dedicating the Kirtland Temple, prayed it should be "established forever." (D&C 109:54.)

"4. May I urge you to seek out good, wise, and honest men for public office, and then support them with your vote. You will note the conditions wherein the Lord counseled that we should support men in political office. They ought to be "good," "wise," and "honest." Some men are good and honest, but not wise. These qualities combined provide statesmanship. I've said it many times: what we need today are men with a mandate higher than the ballot box!

"5. I would urge you to heed strictly the commandments of God, particularly the Ten Commandments. As long as we regard God as our Sovereign and uphold his laws, we shall be free from bondage and be protected from external danger.

"Yes, my brothers and sisters, fellow citizens of this great nation, there are sovereign remedies for the debilitating diseases that are eating away the vitals of our political, social, economic, and religious lives. Those remedies are: keep the commandments of God and uphold the basic principles upon which this country was founded.

"America has a spiritual foundation. But today she stands at the crossroads, The crisis before her is a crisis of faith; the need is for greater spirituality and a return to the basic principles upon which this nation was founded.

"The days ahead are sobering and challenging and will require the faith, prayers, loyalty, and courage of every citizen.

"May God's blessings be upon us that your generation will be equal to the task."[6]

# # #

Recommended Resources:

- Article: *What is Left, What is Right* by W. Cleon Skousen. Find at: latterdayconservative.com

- Article: *America, a Choice Land* by Ezra Taft Benson. Find at: latterdayconservative.com

- Article: *Americans Are Destroying America* by Ezra Taft Benson. Find at: latterdayconservative.com

- Video: *Overview of America* by The John Birch Society. YouTube, TheJohnBirchSociety channel

- Video: *Man, Freedom, Government* by Ezra Taft Benson. YouTube, ldsconservative channel

- Video: *The Three Foundings of America* by Stephen Pratt. YouTube, ldsconservative channel

- Document: *The Declaration of Independence*

THE CONSTITUTION: A HEAVENLY BANNER

The Prophet Joseph Smith said the following about the U.S. Constitution:

"The Constitution, when it says, 'We, the people of the United States, in order to form a more perfect union, establish justice, ensure domestic tranquility, provide for the common defense, promote the general welfare, and secure the blessings of liberty to ourselves and our posterity, do ordain and establish this Constitution for the United States of America,' meant just what it said without reference to color or condition, ad infinitum."[1]

"Hence we say, that the Constitution of the United States is a glorious standard; it is founded in the wisdom of God. It is a heavenly banner; it is to all those who are privileged with the sweets of liberty, like the cooling shades and refreshing waters of a great rock in a thirsty and weary land. It is like a great tree under whose branches men from every clime can be shielded from the burning rays of the sun... We say that God is true; that the

Constitution of the United States is true; that the Bible is true."[2]

To this day, the leaders of the Church of Jesus Christ of Latter-day Saints continue to express the importance of the U.S. Constitution.

Gordon B. Hinckley said:

"[The Constitution] is the keystone of our nation. It is the guarantee of our liberty. That original document, with the Bill of Rights, constitutes the charter of our freedom. Through all of the years that have followed we have had some ambitious men who have sought to subvert the great principles of the Constitution, but somehow we have endured one crisis after another. We have been involved in terrible wars during this, the bloodiest of all centuries in the history of man. All of this is part of the miracle that is America, the struggle, the travail, the bitterness, the jealousies, the cynicism, and the criticism. But beyond and above it all is the wonder of a nation that for more than two centuries has remained free and independent and strong, the envy of the world, the hope of the world, the protection of free men everywhere, the manifestation of the power of the Almighty."

Heber J. Grant said:

"Every faithful Latter-day Saint believes that the Constitution of the United States was inspired of God, and that this choice land and this nation have been preserved until now in the principles of liberty under the protection of God...

"These principles are fundamental to our belief, fundamental to our protection. And in the providence of the Lord, the safeguards which have been incorporated into the basic structure of this nation are, if we preserve them, the guarantee of all men who dwell here against abuses, tyrannies, and usurpations. From my childhood days I have understood that we believe absolutely that the Constitution of our country is an inspired instrument, and that God directed those who created it and those who defended the independence of this nation...

"And such the Constitution of the United States must be to every faithful Latter-day Saint who lives under its protection. That the Lord may help him to think straight, and to pursue a straight course regardless of personal advantage, factional interest, or political persuasion, should be the daily prayer of every Latter-day Saint. I counsel you, I urge you, I plead with you, never, so far as you have voice or influence, permit any departure from the principles of government on which this nation was founded, or any disregard of the freedoms which, by the inspiration of God our Father, were written into the Constitution of the United States."

Unfortunately, today the Constitution is mostly disregarded by those whom the people have chosen to represent them in government. Despite how far we have strayed from the Constitution, and the limitations it was intended to place on government, it is important that we read and understand it. It is important the we only support laws that are in accordance to the Constitution and the principles of righteousness.

Excerpts from Ezra Taft Benson's *The Constitution: A Heavenly Banner*:

"We honor more than those who brought forth the Constitution. We honor the Lord who revealed it. God himself has borne witness to the fact that he is pleased with the final product of the work of these great patriots.

"The Constitution consists of seven separate articles. The first three establish the three branches of our government the legislative, the executive, and the judicial. The fourth article describes matters pertaining to states, most significantly the guarantee of a republican form of government to every state of the Union. Article 5 defines the amendment procedure of the document, a deliberately difficult process that should be clearly understood by every citizen. Article 6 covers several miscellaneous items, including a definition of the supreme law of the land, namely, the Constitution itself. Article 7, the last, explains how the Constitution is to be ratified. After ratification of the document, ten amendments were added and designated as our Bill of Rights.

"Now to look at some of the major provisions of the document itself. Many principles could be examined, but I mention five as being crucial to the preservation of our freedom. If we understand the workability of these, we have taken the first step in defending our freedoms.

"The major provisions of the Constitution are as follows:

Sovereignty of the People

"First: Sovereignty lies in the people themselves. Every governmental system has a sovereign, one or several who possess all the executive, legislative, and judicial powers. That sovereign may be an individual, a group, or the people themselves. The Founding Fathers believed in common law, which holds that true sovereignty rests with the people. Believing this to be in accord with truth, they inserted this imperative in the Declaration of Independence: 'To secure these rights [life, liberty, and the pursuit of happiness], Governments are instituted among Men, deriving their just powers from the consent of the governed.'

Separation of Powers

"Second: To safeguard these rights, the Founding Fathers provided for the separation of powers among the three branches of government-the legislative, the executive, and the judicial. Each was to be independent of the other, yet each was to work in a unified relationship. As the great constitutionalist President J. Reuben Clark noted:

"It is [the] union of independence and dependence of these branches-legislative, executive and judicial – and of the governmental functions possessed by each of them, that constitutes the marvelous genius of this unrivaled document.... It was here that the divine inspiration came. It was truly a miracle.

"The use of checks and balances was deliberately designed, first, to make it difficult for a minority of the people to control the government, and, second, to place restraint on the government itself.

Limited Powers of Government

"Third: The powers the people granted to the three branches of government were specifically limited. The Founding Fathers well understood human nature and its tendency to exercise unrighteous dominion when given authority. A constitution was therefore designed to limit government to certain enumerated functions, beyond which was tyranny.

The Principle of Representation

"Fourth: Our constitutional government is based on the principle of representation. The principle of representation means that we have delegated to an elected official the power to represent us. The

Constitution provides for both direct representation and indirect representation. Both forms of representation provide a tempering influence on pure democracy. The intent was to protect the individual's and the minority's rights to life, liberty, and the fruits of their labors-property. These rights were not to be subject to majority vote.

A Moral and Righteous People

"Fifth: The Constitution was designed to work with only a moral and righteous people. "Our constitution," said John Adams (first vice-president and second president of the United States), "was made only for a moral and religious people. It is wholly inadequate to the government of any other".

"At this bicentennial celebration (1986) we must, with sadness, say that we have not been wise in keeping the trust of our Founding Fathers. For the past two centuries, those who do not prize freedom have chipped away at every major clause of our Constitution until today we face a crisis of great dimensions.

"We are fast approaching that moment prophesied by Joseph Smith when he said: 'Even this Nation will be on the very verge of crumbling to pieces and tumbling to the ground and when the constitution is upon the brink of ruin this people will be the Staff up[on] which the Nation shall lean and they shall bear the constitution away from the very verge of destruction.'

"Will we be prepared? Will we be among those who will "bear the Constitution away from the very verge of destruction"? If we desire to be numbered among those who will, here are some things we must do:

"1. We must be righteous and moral. We must live the gospel principles-all of them. We have no right to expect a higher degree of morality from those who represent us than what we ourselves are. To live a higher law means we will not seek to receive what we have not earned by our own labor. It means we will remember that government owes us nothing. It means we will keep the laws of the land. It means we will look to God as our Lawgiver and the source of our liberty.

"2. We must learn the principles of the Constitution and then abide by its precepts. Have we read the Constitution and pondered it? Are we aware of its principles? Could we defend it? Can we recognize when a law is constitutionally unsound? The Church will not tell us how to do this, but we are admonished to do it. I quote Abraham Lincoln: 'Let [the Constitution] be taught in schools, in seminaries, and in colleges; let it be written in primers, spelling-books, and in almanacs; let it be preached from the pulpit, proclaimed in legislative halls, and enforced in courts of justice. And, in short, let it become the political religion of the nation.'

"3. We must become involved in civic affairs. As citizens of this republic, we cannot do our duty and be idle spectators. It is vital that we follow this counsel from the Lord: "Honest men and wise men should be sought for diligently, and good men and wise men ye should observe to uphold; otherwise whatsoever is less than these cometh of evil" (D&C 98:10). Note the qualities that the Lord demands in those who are to represent us. They must be good, wise, and honest. We must be concerted in our desires and efforts to see men and women represent us who possess all three of these qualities.

"4. We must make our influence felt by our vote, our letters, and our advice. We must be wisely informed and let others know how we feel. We must take part in local precinct meetings and select delegates who will truly represent our feelings.

"I have faith that the Constitution will be saved as prophesied by Joseph Smith. But it will not be saved in Washington. It will be saved by the citizens of this nation who love and cherish freedom. It will be saved by enlightened members of this Church – men and women who will subscribe to and abide by the principles of the Constitution."[5]

# # #

Recommended Resources:

- Article: *The Constitution - A Heavenly* Banner by Ezra Taft Benson. Find at: latterdayconservative.com

- Article: *101 Constitutional Questions to Ask Candidates* by W. Cleon Skousen. See: latterdayconservative.com

- Article: *Christ and the Constitution* by Ezra Taft Benson. Find at: latterdayconservative.com

- Video: *The Constitution: A Heavenly Banner* by Ezra Taft Benson. YouTube, ldsconservative channel

- Video: *Original Intent* by Stephen Pratt. YouTube, ldsconservative channel

- Document: *Constitution of United States of America.* See: constitutionus.com

FREEDOM AND FREE ENTERPRISE

Today, capitalism is regarded by many as a *bad* and oppressive system and unfortunately this view is perpetuated in many of the educational institutions throughout the nation. Unfortunately, many corporations have also been doing terrible things that get labelled as capitalism but that is not true free-market capitalism.

"Capitalism is a social system based on the principle of individual rights. Politically, it is the system of laissez-faire (freedom). Legally it is a system of objective laws (rule of law as opposed to rule of man). Economically, when such freedom is applied to the sphere of production its result is the free-market." (source: capitalism.org)

This lesson presents a view of free enterprise, moral, principle-based capitalism that we desperately need more and more people to understand and practice in America and throughout the world.

Quoting from Ayn Rand, author of *Atlas Shrugged, Capitalism: The Unknown Ideal,* and other books:

"No politico-economic system in history has ever proved its value so eloquently or has benefited mankind so greatly as capitalism—and none has ever been attacked so savagely, viciously, and blindly. The flood of misinformation, misrepresentation, distortion, and outright falsehood about capitalism is such that the young people of today have no idea (and virtually no way of discovering any idea) of its actual nature.

"...By their silence—by their evasion of the clash between capitalism and altruism—it is capitalism's alleged champions who are responsible for the fact that capitalism is being destroyed without a hearing, without a trial, without any public knowledge of its principles, its nature, its history, or its moral meaning. It is being destroyed in the manner of a nightmare lynching—as if a blind, despair-crazed mob were burning a straw man, not knowing that the grotesquely deformed bundle of straw is hiding the living body of the ideal.

"The method of capitalism's destruction rests on never letting the world discover what it is that is being destroyed—on never allowing it to be identified within the hearing of the young."[1]

The Founders generally believed that America should be organized in a way that allows people the freedom to pursue and obtain the basic necessities of life. The idea of the American Dream is that anyone could become a commercial success. Essentially this is what we call a free-market or free-enterprise system.

Hamilton wanted to have a society where everyone is working for big entities and organizations, big industry in which a lot of people are working together to create wealth. As you can see today we're seeing more and more of this, and less and less of what Jefferson promoted.

Jefferson recognized this would limit the people's freedom. The model Jefferson proposed is having a bunch of people who are farmers, land owners, shop owners, businessmen and entrepreneurs. People who are more independent rather than dependent.

The Law of the Harvest

Excerpts from Howard W. Hunter's BYU devotional speech *The Law of the Harvest*:

"The primary responsibility for your education is yours. It is not the Church's; it is not the administrators' responsibility; it is not even your teachers' – it is yours. To the degree you accept this responsibility and are diligent in discharging it, you will succeed, you will grow and develop an educated mind and an educated heart. As you are true to the laws of God you will develop a divine character. To the degree that you do not accept this responsibility you will not grow and develop within.

"People grow mentally, socially, emotionally, and spiritually only to the degree they obey on a daily basis the laws governing such growth.

"The Lord tells us clearly and powerfully: "There is a law, irrevocably decreed in heaven before the foundations of this world, upon which all blessings are predicated – And when we obtain any blessing from God, it is by obedience to that law upon which it is predicated." (D&C 130:20-21.)

"What is true with an individual is also true with a nation. You can absolutely rely on this – a nation cannot violate basic principles with impunity, that is, without paying the awful price, any more than an individual can violate basic principles with impunity.

"We hear a lot of economic and political arguments going on around the country today. We have for a long time. Words like *socialism, free enterprise, the welfare state, states rights, federal control, human rights, property rights, communism*, are bantered around widely. You may wonder what these words mean. I wonder myself because they are used with such varieties of meaning. Often in your search to understand them you run into a barrage of more such words and even prejudice and bull-headedness, and you come out of the fray more confused and more frustrated. I believe much of this can be simplified.

"You were given a great message by Elder Marion G. Romney which was inspiring and profound. He compared socialism with the United Order. I encourage you to study carefully that message. He gave much of the basic theory, the principles, the similarities and the differences between these two basically conflicting systems. The basic principle in his message is the same principle in mine, as already discussed – the principle of *the Law of the Harvest – As a Man Sows, So Shall He Reap.*

"From my own experience in business and as a lawyer and church worker, and from my firsthand observations in this country and other countries of the world, there appears to me to be a trend to shift responsibility for life and its processes from the individual to the state. In this shift there is a basic violation of the Law of the Harvest, or the law of justice. The attitude of "something for nothing" is encouraged. The government is often looked to as the source of wealth. There is the feeling that the government should step in and take care of one's needs, one's emergencies, and one's future.

"The right to own and control private property is not only a human right; it is a divine right. We will largely be judged, if I understand the Savior's teachings correctly (see Matthew 25), by how we use our property voluntarily for the blessings and benefit of our Father's other children. President McKay continually teaches us that this right of free agency is our most precious heritage. It is our greatest gift in this world and is to be valued even more than life itself.

"If you deprive a man of his right to fail in the righteous use of his property, you also deprive him of his right to succeed. If you remove from a man his right to "go to hell," you likewise remove his free agency to go to heaven. Satan's entire philosophy is based on a "something for nothing" philosophy: salvation without effort – a free gift. This counterfeit doctrine was rejected by God our Father. Our Elder Brother, Jesus Christ, accepted our Father's plan and agreed to pay the infinite price to become our Savior and Redeemer and to show us the way back to the Father. The way is often the hard way. It is the Law of the Harvest. It is the same basic law in the spiritual realm which the farmer must obey in the physical realm. He plants in the spring and cultivates, waters, weeds, and nourishes the ground and its new life and then harvests in the fall.

"What is the real cause of this trend toward the welfare state, toward more socialism? In the last analysis, in my judgment, it is personal unrighteousness. When people do not use their freedoms responsibly and righteously, they will gradually lose these freedoms.

"Let me illustrate: If I, as an employer, in my policies and practices exploit my employees, I will either lose them and my business, or my employees will gather together and threaten to strike me. They will strive to exercise an influence on the legislative process so that laws will be enacted dictating fair employment policies and practices, thus limiting my freedom to determine these things for myself.

"If man will not recognize the inequalities around him and voluntarily, through the gospel plan, come to the aid of his brother, as outlined by Brother Romney, he will find that through "a democratic process" he will be forced to come to the aid of his brother. The government will take from the "haves" and give to the "have nots." Both have lost their freedom. Those who "have," lost their freedom to give voluntarily of their own free will and in the way they desire. Those who "have not" lost their freedom because they did not earn what they received. They got "something for nothing," and they will neither appreciate the gift nor the giver of the gift.

"The only way we can keep our freedom is through our personal righteousness – by handling that freedom responsibly. We are our brother's keeper. We must be concerned for the social problems of today. We must take that responsibility upon ourselves according to the gospel plan but not according to the socialistic plan.

"You know that it is vain and foolish for a doctor to criticize the symptoms of a disease and refuse to work upon the roots. So, also, it is superficial to only criticize socialism and the welfare state and the many other evil "isms" growing up among us unless we work upon the roots. It is only in the changing of a man's heart – a second birth – the changing of an individual, that the root strength comes to change a people or a nation."[2]

It is recommended that you read Howard W. Hunter's *The Law of the Harvest* speech in its entirety. It can be found on the website: latterdayconservative.com

Ezra Taft Benson also spoke at length about *freedom and free enterprise.* Below are some excerpts from the talk.

"Far too many today are enjoying a comfortable complacency. We are a prosperous nation, our people have high paying jobs, our incomes are high, our standard of living is at an unprecedented level. We do not like to be disturbed as we enjoy our life of ease. We live in the soft present and feel the future is secure. We do not worry about history. We seem oblivious to the causes to the rises and falls of nations. We are blind to the hard fact that nations usually sow the seeds of their own destruction while enjoying unprecedented prosperity. I say to you with all the fervor of my soul, we are sowing the seeds of our own destruction in America and much of the free world today.

"It is my sober warning to you today that if the trends of the past forty years and especially the last fifteen years continue we will lose that which is as priceless as life itself: our freedom, our liberty, our right to act as free men. It can happen here, it is happening here. The outlook for free enterprise in the world has never seemed so uncertain as now. (*note: this message was originally given in 1977*)

"Do we as American citizens have the desire and will for capitalism, and free enterprise to survive?

"Today it seems evident that we are rearing a generation of Americans who do not understand the productive base of our society and how we came by such prosperity. Evidence of this fact is found in surveys taken among some of our high school and college students. The majority of whom it is reported believe private enterprise is a failure. Although they don't have a clear understanding of what private enterprise is. With them as with many adults there is a vague notion that it is some unfair system which stands to give special advantage to big corporations and wealthy individuals.

"Many of you see the idea of the free enterprise or the free market system as only an alternative economic system to our other systems. This is a serious oversight and causes many to miss the most crucial element to the free market system. May I mention some of these features?

- The free market system rests on a moral base.
- The free market is based on the right to property.
- The free market is based on the right to enjoy private enterprise for profit.
- The free market is the right to voluntary exchange of goods and services, free from

restraints and controls.

- A free market survives with competition.

"A free market society recognizes private property as sacred because the individual is entitled to ownership of goods and property which he has earned; he is sovereign so far as human law is concerned over his own goods. He may retain possession of his goods; he may pass his wealth on to his family or to charitable causes. For one cannot give what one does not own.

"James Madison recognized that property consisted not only of man's external goods, his land, merchandise and money, but more sacredly he had title to his thoughts, opinions, and conscience. The civil government's obligation then is to safeguard this right and to frame laws which secure to every man the free exercise of his conscience and the right and control of his property. No liberty is possible except a man is protected in his title to his legal holdings and property and can be indemnified by the law for its loss or destruction. Remove this right and man is reduced to serfdom. Former United States Supreme Court Justice George Southerland said it this way. 'To give man liberty but take from him the property which is the fruit and badge of his liberty is to still leave him a slave.'

"Nothing is more to be prized, nor more sacred than man's free choice. Free choice is the essence of free enterprise. It recognizes that the common man will make choices in his own self-interest. It allows the manufacturer to produce what he wants, how much, and to set his own price. It allows the buyer to decide if he wants a certain product at the price established. It preserves the right to work when and where we choose.

"When government presumes to demand more and more of the fruits of a man's labor through taxation and reduces more and more his actual income by printing money and furthering debt, the wage earner is left with less and less to buy food, to provide housing, medical care, education and private welfare. The individuals are left without a choice and must look to the state as its benevolent supporter of these services. When that happens liberty is gone.

"Economic literacy among our people has not been one of the bright spots in our 200 year old history. Yet it is apparent that when ignorance prevails the people eventually suffer. The principles behind our American free market economy can be reduced to a rather simple formula. Here it is, and I hope if you forget everything else I said, you'll remember this formula. It is so basic and so simple.

Free Market Economy's Simple Formula:

1. Economic security for all is impossible without widespread abundance.

2. Abundance is impossible without industrious and ambitious production.

3. Such production is impossible without energetic, willing and eager labor.

4. This labor is not possible without incentive.

5. Of all forms of incentive, the freedom to obtain a reward for ones labors is the most sustaining for most people, sometimes called the "profit motive". It is simply the right to plan and to earn, and to enjoy the fruits of your labor.

6. This profit motive diminishes as government controls, regulations and taxes increase to deny the fruits of success to those who produce.

7. Therefore any attempt through government intervention to redistribute the material rewards of labor can only result in the eventual destruction of the productive base of society, without which real abundance and security for more than the ruling elite is quite impossible.

"The best way, the American way, is still maximum freedom for the individual guaranteed by a wise government that provides for the police department and national defense. History records that eventually people get the form of government they deserve. Good government which guarantees the maximum of freedom, liberty, and development of the individual must be based upon sound principles. We must ever remember that ideas and principles are either sound or unsound in spite of those who hold them. Freedom of achievement has produced and will continue to produce the maximum of benefits in terms of human welfare. Freedom is an eternal principle. Heaven disapproves of force, coercion and intimidation. Only a free people can be truly a happy people.

"Of all sad things in the world, the saddest in the world is to see the people who have once known liberty and freedom and then lost it.

"I leave with you this challenge that you help others see that the real issue is not over economic systems, it is the issue of freedom and limited or no freedom, the same issue that brought about this nation's birth and independence. Yes, with God's help and inspiration perhaps we may rekindle a flame of liberty that will last as long as time endures."[3]

# # #

Recommended Resources:

- Article: *Freedom and Free Enterprise* by Ezra Taft Benson. Find at: latterdayconservative.com

- Video: *Freedom and Free Enterprise* by Ezra Taft Benson. YouTube, ldsconservative channel

- Article: *The Law of the Harvest* by Howard W. Hunter. Find at: latterdayconservative.com

- Video: *Equality and Freedom in the Free Enterprise System* by Milton Friedman. YouTube, Free To Choose Network channel

WAR AND FOREIGN POLICY

War and foreign policy are complex and often controversial topics. Even among liberty-minded individuals, it is not uncommon to come across disputes about the various wars the United States has been involved in and whether those wars were justified. Some would argue that very few of the wars the U.S. has been involved in were justified.

In modern scriptures the Lord tells us what is required for a war to be considered justified:

"Renounce war and proclaim peace... And again, this is the law that I gave unto mine ancients, that they should not go out unto battle against any nation, kindred, tongue, or people, save I, the Lord, commanded them. And if any nation, tongue, or people should proclaim war against them, they should first lift a standard of peace unto that people, nation, or tongue; and if that people did not accept the offering of peace, neither the second nor the third time, they should bring these testimonies before the Lord; then I, the Lord, would give unto them a commandment, and justify them in going out to battle against that nation, tongue, or people.

And I, the Lord, would fight their battles, and their children's battles, and their children's children's, until they had avenged themselves on all their enemies, to the third and fourth generation. Behold, this is an ensample unto all people, saith the Lord your God, for justification before me.

"And again, verily I say unto you, if after thine enemy has come upon thee the first time, he repent and come unto thee praying thy forgiveness, thou shalt forgive him, and shalt hold it no more as a testimony against thine enemy.." (D&C 98.)

The Book of Mormon also gives examples of what constitutes an unjust war (showing justification for defensive war and forbidding offensive war):

"Now the people said unto Gidgiddoni: Pray unto the Lord, and let us go up upon the mountains and into the wilderness, that we may fall upon the robbers and destroy them in their own lands. But Gidgiddoni saith unto them: The Lord forbid; for if we should go up against them the Lord would deliver us into their hands; therefore we will prepare ourselves in the center of our lands, and we will gather all our armies together, and we will not go against them, but we will wait till they shall come against us; therefore as the Lord liveth, if we do this he will deliver them into our hands." (3 Nephi 3: 18–21.)

"And it was because the armies of the Nephites went up unto the Lamanites that they began to be smitten; for were it not for that, the Lamanites could have had no power over them. But, behold, the judgments of God will overtake the wicked; and it is by the wicked that the wicked are punished; for it is the wicked that stir up the hearts of the children of men unto bloodshed." (Mormon 4: 4-5.)

Spencer W. Kimball, in a 1976 *First Presidency Message* titled *The False Gods We Worship*, said the following:

"In spite of our delight in defining ourselves as modern, and our tendency to think we possess a sophistication that no people in the past ever had—in spite of these things, we are, on the whole, an idolatrous people—a condition most repugnant to the Lord.

"We are a warlike people, easily distracted from our assignment of preparing for the coming of the Lord. When enemies rise up, we commit vast resources to the fabrication of gods of stone and steel—ships, planes, missiles, fortifications—and depend on them for protection and deliverance. When threatened, we become anti-enemy instead of pro-kingdom of God; we train a man in the art of war and call him a patriot, thus, in the manner of Satan's counterfeit of true patriotism, perverting the Savior's teaching:

"'Love your enemies, bless them that curse you, do good to them that hate you, and pray for them which despitefully use you, and persecute you; that ye may be the children of your Father which is in heaven.' (Matt. 5:44–45.)

"We forget that if we are righteous the Lord will either not suffer our enemies to come upon us—and this is the special promise to the inhabitants of the land of the Americas (see 2 Ne. 1:7)—or he will fight our battles for us (Ex. 14:14; D&C 98:37, to name only two references of many)."[1]

W. Cleon Skousen wrote about the *war powers and the remaining enumerated powers*:

"One of the most important reasons the states united together was to promote their mutual defense. Spelling out the war powers was therefore a highly significant segment of the Constitution.

"It will be noted that the entire depository of power in connection with the military was vested in the Congress, not the President. This meant that Congress had to declare war before the President could take action. An exception, of course, was allowed in the case of an unexpected invasion, authorizing the President to take emergency action as commander in chief of the armed services.

"In the Constitutional Convention there was strong opposition to a standing army. The entire army was demobilized just as soon as the Revolutionary War was finished. The Founders did not want the President to have the power to raise an army as the British kings had repeatedly done.

Furthermore, they did not want the Congress to vest the President with permanent funds to support the military. Their object was to prevent both the President and the Congress from setting up a structure which might become a military dictatorship."[2]

Thomas Jefferson said the following about war:

"We love and we value peace; we know its blessings from experience. We abhor the follies of war, and are not untried in its distresses and calamities. Unmeddling with the affairs of other nations, we had hoped that our distance and our dispositions would have left us free in the example and indulgence of peace with all the world... We confide in our strength without boasting of it; we respect that of others without fearing it."[3]

Benjamin Franklin felt that war was a terrible waste:

"In my opinion, there never was a good war or a bad peace. What vast additions to the conveniences and comforts of living might mankind have acquired if the money spent in wars had been employed in works of public utility! What an extension of agriculture, even to the tops of our mountains; what rivers rendered navigable, or joined by canals; what bridges, aqueducts, new roads, and other public works, edifices, and improvements, rendering a ... complete paradise, might have been obtained by spending those millions in doing good which in the last war have been spent in doing mischief; in bringing misery into thousands of families, and destroying the lives of so many thousands of working people, who might have performed the useful labor!"[4]

James Madison believed that a standing army is a dangerous but necessary provision:

"A standing force ... is a dangerous ... necessary, provision. On the smallest scale it has its inconveniences. On an extensive scale its consequences may be fatal...

"The Union itself ... destroys every pretext for a military establishment which could be dangerous. America united, with a handful of troops, or without a single soldier, exhibits a more forbidding posture to foreign ambition than America disunited, with a hundred thousand veterans ready for combat... A dangerous establishment can never be necessary or plausible, so long as they continue a united people. But let it never for a moment be forgotten that they are indebted for this advantage to the Union alone. The moment of its dissolution will be the date of a new order of things...

"Next to the effectual establishment of the Union, the best possible precaution against danger from standing armies is a limitation of the term for which revenue may be appropriated to their support. This precaution the Constitution has prudently added."[5]

George Washington made the following statement in his Farewell Address:

"Observe good faith and justice towards all Nations; cultivate peace and harmony with all. Religion and Morality enjoin this conduct; and can it be, that good policy does not equally enjoin it? It will be worthy of a free, enlightened, and, at no distant period, a great Nation, to give to mankind the magnanimous and too novel example of a people always guided by an exalted justice and benevolence. Who can doubt, that, in the course of time and things, the fruits of such a plan would richly repay any temporary advantages, which might be lost by a steady adherence to it ? Can it be, that Providence has not connected the permanent felicity of a Nation with its Virtue? The experiment, at least, is recommended by every sentiment which ennobles human nature. Alas! is it rendered impossible by its vices?"[6]

Ezra Taft Benson spoke the following words of wisdom regarding United States Foreign Policy:

"Ever since World War I, when we sent American boys to Europe supposedly to "make the world safe for democracy", our leaders in Washington have been acting as though the American people elected them to office for the primary purpose of leading the entire planet toward international peace, prosperity and one-world government.

"...We mistake the object of our government...

Conquest or superiority among other powers is not or ought not ever to be the object of republican systems. If they are sufficiently active and energetic to rescue us from contempt and preserve our domestic happiness and security, it is all we can expect from them...

"There is one and only one legitimate goal of United States foreign policy. It is a narrow goal, a nationalistic goal: the preservation of our national independence. Nothing in the Constitution grants that the President shall have the privilege of offering himself as a world leader.

"Nothing in the Constitution nor in logic grants to the President of the United States or to Congress the power to influence the political life of other countries, to "uplift" their cultures, to bolster their economies, to feed their peoples or even to defend them against their enemies.

"The preservation of America's political, economic and military independence–the three cornerstones of sovereignty–is the sum and total prerogative of our government in dealing with the affairs of the world. Beyond that point, any humanitarian or charitable activities are the responsibility of individual citizens voluntarily without coercion of others to participate.

"The proper function of government must be limited to a defensive role–the defense of individual citizens against bodily harm, theft and involuntary servitude at the hands of either domestic or foreign criminals. But to protect our people from bodily harm at the hands of foreign aggressors, we must maintain a military force which is not only capable of crushing an invasion, but of striking a sufficiently powerful counter-blow as to make in unattractive for would-be conquerors to try their luck with us.

"Should we enter into treaties such as the U.N. Covenants which would obligate our citizens to conform their social behavior, their educational practices to rules and regulations set down by international agencies? Such treaty obligations amount to the voluntary and piece-meal surrender of our political independence.

"We must put off our rose-colored glasses, quit repeating those soothing but entirely false statements about world unity and brotherhood, and look to the world as it is, not as we would like it to become. Such an objective, and perhaps painful, survey leads to but one conclusion. We would be committing national suicide to surrender any of our independence, and chain ourselves to other nations in such a sick and turbulent world.

"Senator Robert A. Taft clearly explained our traditional foreign policy:

"'Our traditional policy of neutrality and non-interference with other nations was based on the principle that this policy was the best way to avoid disputes with other nations and to maintain the liberty of this country without war. From the days of George Washington that has been the policy of the United States. It has never been isolationism; but it has always avoided alliances and interference in foreign quarrels as a preventive against possible war, and it has always opposed any commitment by the United States, in advance, to take any military action outside of our territory. It would leave us free to interfere or not according to whether we consider the case of sufficiently vital interest to the liberty of this country. It was the policy of the free hand.'

"Many well-intentioned people are now convinced that we are living in a period of history which makes it both possible and necessary to abandon our national sovereignty, to merge our nation militarily, economically, and politically with other nations, and to form, at last a world government which, supposedly, would put an end to war... But such an evaluation is a shallow one.

"There are two kinds of peace. If we define peace as merely the absence of war, then we could be talking about the peace that reigns in a communist slave labor camp. The wretched souls in prison there are not at war, but do you think they would call it peace?

"The only real peace – the one most of us think about when we use the term – is a peace with freedom. A Nation that is not willing, if necessary, to face the rigors of war to defend its real peace-in-freedom is doomed to lose both its freedom and its peace! These are the hard facts of life. We may not like them, but until we live in a far better world than exists today, we must face up to them squarely and courageously.

"Until all nations follow the concept of limited government, it is unlikely that universal peace will ever be realized on this planet. Unlimited, power-grasping governments will always resort to force if they think they can get away with it."[7]

In that same talk, Benson also shared the following general principles regarding war and foreign policy:

- Establish and maintain a position of independence with regard to other countries
- Avoid political connection, involvement or intervention in the affairs of other countries
- Make no permanent or entangling alliances
- Treat all nations impartially, neither granting nor accepting special privileges from any
- Promote commerce with all free peoples and countries
- Cooperate with other countries to develop civilized rules of intercourse
- Act always in accordance with the "laws of Nations"
- Remedy all just claims of injury to other nations and require just treatment from other nations, standing ready, if necessary to punish offenders
- Maintain a defensive force of sufficient

magnitude to deter aggressors.

# # #

Recommended Resources:

- Article: *United States Foreign Policy* by Ezra Taft Benson. Find at: latterdayconservative.com

- Article: *The False Gods We Worship* by Spencer W. Kimball. Find at: latterdayconservative.com

- Article: *The War Powers and the Remaining Enumerated Powers* by W. Cleon Skousen. Find at: latterdayconservative.com

- Video: *War & Current Events* by Jack Monnett. YouTube, ldsconservative channel

- Video: Search for *Ron Paul Foreign Policy* videos on YouTube, various channels

THE HIDDEN THINGS
OF DARKNESS:
POLITICAL SECRET
COMBINATIONS

This lesson is not meant to expose specific individuals or groups that are part of the conspiracy but is intended as a warning that such secret combinations do exist – even today – and they seek to overthrow the freedom of all nations and people. At the end of this lesson there are several additional recommended resources that explore more specific details of the conspiracy. In many ways the people are to blame for the corruption and tolerance of tyranny and injustice in America – *we sow the seeds of our own destruction.* There are also people who work in darkness behind the scenes to influence the course of the nation, whether directly or indirectly. We know that these secret combinations exist, even today, and it has been prophesied in the scriptures:

"It is wisdom in God that these things should be shown unto you, that thereby ye may repent of your sins, and suffer not that these murderous combinations shall get above you, which are built up to get power and gain—and the work, yea, even the work of destruction come upon you, yea, even the sword of the justice of the Eternal God shall fall upon you, to your overthrow and destruction if ye shall suffer these things to be. Wherefore, the Lord commandeth you, when ye shall see these things come among you that ye shall awake to a sense of your awful situation, because of this secret combination which shall be among you... whoso buildeth it up seeketh to overthrow the freedom of all lands, nations, and countries; and it bringeth to pass the destruction of all people, for it is built up by the devil, who is the father of all lies..." (Book of Mormon, Ether 8.)

Ezra Taft Benson warned us on multiple occasions, in General Conference, about these secret combinations:

"Joseph Smith said that the Book of Mormon was the 'keystone of our religion' and the 'most correct' book on earth. This most correct book on earth states that the downfall of two great American civilizations came as a result of secret conspiracies whose desire was to overthrow the freedom of the people. 'And they have caused the destruction of this people of whom I am now speaking,' says Moroni, 'and also the destruction of the people of Nephi.'

"Now undoubtedly Moroni could have pointed out many factors that led to the destruction of the people, but notice how he singled out the secret combinations, just as the Church today could point out many threats to peace, prosperity, and the spread of God's work, but it has singled out the greatest threat as the godless conspiracy. There is no conspiracy theory in the Book of Mormon — it is a conspiracy fact.

"And along this line, I would highly recommend to you a new book entitled *None Dare Call it Conspiracy*, by Gary Allen."[1]

These problems are not just on a national level and they haven't gone away since the warnings from Ezra Taft Benson. A few individuals in an organization called Defending Utah have been hard at work researching and discovering solid evidence of Utah's Secret Combinations. There have been forces at work in Utah with the apparent goal of preventing Zion and leading us more and more into Babylon. The conspiracy has been accomplished via means of government, politics, political parties and through the public education system.

John Taylor acknowledged the existence of the conspiracy in Utah:

"The scenes which we are now witnessing in this territory are the results of a deep-laid and carefully planned conspiracy, which has been in process of formation for years. Its originators knew the elements they had to deal with, and by cunning contrivance they have effected a wonderful combination... Each is made to believe that it is to his direct interest to combine to destroy Mormonism."[2]

In 1961, Ezra Taft Benson gave a talk in General Conference further identifying the secret combination in America:

"The world-wide secret conspiracy which has risen up in our day to fulfil these prophecies is easily identified. President McKay has left no room for doubt as to what attitude Latter-day Saints should take toward the modern "secret combinations" of conspiratorial communism. In a lengthy statement on communism, he said:

'. . . Latter-day Saints should have nothing to do with the secret combinations and groups antagonistic to the constitutional law of the land, which the Lord *suffered to be established*, and which *should be maintained for the rights and protection of all flesh according to just and holy principles.*'[3]

"What is the official position of the Church on communism? In 1936 the First Presidency made an official declaration on communism which has never been abrogated. I quote the concluding paragraph:

'We call upon all Church members completely to eschew communism. The safety of our divinely inspired constitutional government and the welfare of our Church imperatively demand that communism shall have no place in America'"[4]

Some might declare that "the war against communism is over, and we won", but the reality is that the threat against our freedom still exists and has had much success in the many years since Ezra Taft Benson gave that talk. It becomes more apparent in some of the additional comments Benson made in that same talk:

"We must ever keep in mind that collectivized socialism is part of the communist strategy. Communism is fundamentally socialism. We will never win our fight against communism by making concessions to socialism. Communism and socialism, closely related, must be defeated on principle. The close relationship between socialism and communism is clearly pointed out by Senator Strom Thurmond of South Carolina in a letter to the editor of the Washington Post, of August 6, 1961, in these words:

'...Both socialism and communism derive from the teachings of Marx and Engels. In fact, the movements were one until the split over methods of approach, which resulted after the Russian revolution in 1905.... The aim and purpose of both was then and is now world socialism, which communism seeks to achieve through revolution and which socialists seek to achieve through evolution.

'The industrial achievements of the U. S. are

the result of an economic system which is the antithesis of socialism. Our economic system is called 'capitalism' or 'private enterprise' and is based on private property rights, the profit motive and competition.

'Both communism and socialism seek to destroy our economic system and replace it with socialism; and their success, whether through evolution by socialism or through revolution by communism or a combination, will destroy not only our economic system, but our liberty, including the 'civil' aspects as well...'

"When socialism is understood, we will realize that many of the programs advocated, and some of those already adopted in the United States, fall clearly within the category of socialism. What is socialism? It is simply governmental ownership and management of the essential means for the production and distribution of goods.

"We must never forget that nations may sow the seeds of their own destruction while enjoying unprecedented prosperity.

"The socialistic-communist conspiracy to weaken the United States involves attacks on many fronts. To weaken the American free-enterprise economy which outproduced both its enemies and allies during World War II is a high priority target of the communist leaders. Their press and other propaganda media are therefore constantly selling the principles of centralized or federal control of farms, railroads, electric power, schools, steel, maritime shipping, and many other aspects of the economy–but always in the name of public welfare.

"This carries out the strategy laid down by the communist masters. John Strachey, a top official in the Labor Socialist party of Great Britain, in his book entitled The Theory and Practice of Socialism said:

'It is impossible to establish communism as the immediate successor to capitalism. It is accordingly proposed to establish socialism as something which we can put in the place of our present decaying capitalism. Hence, communists work for the establishment of socialism as a necessary transition stage on the road to communism.'"

In the August 2005 Ensign, President Gordon B. Hinckley exhorted the Members to read the Book of Mormon by the end of year and stated:

"The Book of Mormon narrative is a chronicle of nations long since gone. But in its descriptions of the problems of today's society, it is as current as the morning newspaper and much more definitive, inspired, and inspiring concerning the solutions of those problems.

"I know of no other writing which sets forth with such clarity the tragic consequences to societies that follow courses contrary to the commandments of God. Its pages trace the stories of two distinct civilizations that flourished on the Western Hemisphere. Each began as a small nation, its people walking in the fear of the Lord. But with prosperity came growing evils. The people succumbed to the wiles of ambitious and scheming leaders who oppressed them with burdensome taxes, who lulled them with hollow promises, who countenanced and even encouraged loose and lascivious living. These evil schemers led the people into terrible wars that resulted in the death of millions and the final and total extinction of two great civilizations in two different eras."

In the last talk he gave in General Conference, Ezra Taft Benson testified of the continued threat of secret combinations:

"I testify that wickedness is rapidly expanding in every segment of our society. It is more highly organized, more cleverly disguised, and more powerfully promoted than ever before. Secret combinations lusting for power, gain, and glory are flourishing. A secret combination that seeks to overthrow the freedom of all lands, nations, and countries is increasing its evil influence and control over America and the entire world."[5]

To conclude this lesson, I will quote from an article entitled *The 11th Commandment of the Book of Mormon*:

"The question arises, 'Even if this is true, what am I supposed to do about it?' I don't believe one can really answer that question until they know that IT IS TRUE. And the ONLY way you're going to find out that it's true is by careful study of the evidence of the secret combinations themselves. Consider the council given in D&C 123: 12–15:

'For there are many yet on the earth among all sects, parties, and denominations, who are blinded by the subtle craftiness of men, whereby they lie in wait to deceive, and who are only kept from the truth because they know not where to find it— Therefore, that we should waste and wear out our lives in bringing to light all the hidden things of darkness, wherein we know them; and they are truly manifest from heaven— These should then be attended to with great earnestness. Let no man count them as small things; for there is much which lieth in futurity, pertaining to the saints, which depends upon these things.'"[6]

# # #

Recommended Resources:

- Book: *The Hidden Things of* Darkness by Christopher S. Bentley. Available at: ldsfreedombooks.com

- Organization: *Defending Utah*. Website: defendingutah.org

- Book: *Awakening to Our Awful Situation* by Jack Monnett. Available at: ldsfreedombooks.com

- Video: *Which Father Are You Following?* by Stephen Pratt. YouTube, ldsconservative channel

- Video: *Awakening to Our Awful Situation*, multiple videos. YouTube, ldsconservative channel

OPPOSITION IN ALL THINGS: SPIRITUAL SECRET COMBINATIONS

The previous lesson focused on political secret combinations. Knowing that such threats exist politically, it should also be obvious that the conspiracy works on a variety of fronts to implement its agenda – through government, education, science, business, religion, etc. This lesson focuses on the spiritual secret combination.

Satan, appearing as an angel of light, is deceiving many people today. Satan's argument in the war in heaven must have seemed so good, so true and right that his followers honestly believed it was the better way – after all, these were spirits who dwelt in the presence of God, the Father; they are his children. Even today Satan continues to deceive, causing many, even those professing to follow Christ, to embrace false principles, and to call evil good and good evil.

Usually when we think of the temptations of the devil, it is in regards to doing that which the world commonly recognizes as bad, such as stealing, lying, murder, and all manners of vices. What is not as frequently spoken of, and often unrecognized, is how Lucifer is deceiving people today, appearing as an angel of light. Satan's deceptions in this manner are often confused as being good, yet one of the keys in recognizing such deceptions is that these paths do not lead to Christ. For there is only one path to Christ and it is straight and narrow.

What are spiritual secret combinations?

Spiritual secret combinations would be those things that could be considered counterfeits to the true Gospel of Jesus Christ. This includes teachings found in many religions, even sometimes within Christianity itself. One of the primary counterfeit gospels gaining popularity today is associated with the new age movement (you may have heard of The Secret, The Law of Attraction, etc.). Early Mormon church leaders referred to it as spiritualism. This is nothing new, simply a "re-branding" of what the Latter-day Saints recognized was taking root since the restoration of the Church of Jesus Christ in modern times. This is not to say that everything associated with that movement is wrong but there is a side to the new age movement that is a counterfeit of the truth. From the time of Adam and Eve, Lucifer has presented his false doctrine to man.

Joseph F. Smith said that:

"Spiritualism started in the United States about the time that Joseph Smith received his visions from the heavens. What more natural than that Lucifer should begin revealing himself to men in his cunning way, in order to deceive them and to distract their minds from the truth that God was revealing? And he has kept it up pretty well ever since."[1]

According to James E. Talmage:

"The restoration of the Priesthood to earth in this age of the world was followed by a phenomenal growth of the vagaries of spiritualism, whereby many were led to put their trust in Satan's counterfeit of God's eternal power."[2]

If Jesus Christ **is** "the way, the truth, and the life" and no one can get to God the Father except through Christ, then it would stand to reason that religions that do not recognize this as truth are part of the counterfeit, albeit possibly innocently. The *New Age movement* promotes a worship of self ("God is within you") and freedom from guilt ("there is no such thing as sin"). It also teaches the *Law of Attraction* which is in contradiction to the *Law of the Harvest*.

In preface to sharing a related story in his book, *No More Strangers, Volume 3*, Elder Hartman Rector stated:

"Members of the Church are warned to carefully keep the commandments of God and are told that then spiritual experiences will come as a result of their faith and their need. These experiences will come from God and not from the adversary. But when people who are not in condition to receive communication from the Lord, court the spirit of the devil by literally seeking "spiritual" experiences, they place themselves in jeopardy every hour to be "sifted as wheat." These experiences cannot be credited to the Lord or considered to be to the good of the individual. All forms of spiritualism are subject to control by Satan, from fortune-telling to transcendental meditation, etc., and should be avoided as we would avoid the plague.

"After much false wandering through the spiritualism maze, Ruth Stevens finally came home to the restored Church of Jesus Christ and its truth. That truth reveals all other systems in their real colors, including those whose black foundation is of Satan.

"This account is deliberately given in some detail so that readers may be made aware of the dangers of seeking "spiritual" experiences outside of the gospel pattern..."

James E. Talmage said:

"Satan has shown himself to be an accomplished strategist and a skillful imitator; the most deplorable of his victories are due to his simulation of good, whereby the undiscerning have been led captive. Let no one be deluded with the thought that any act, the immediate result of which appears to be benign, is necessarily productive of permanent good. It may serve the dark purposes of Satan to play upon the human sense of goodness, even to the extent of healing the body and apparently of thwarting death."[3]

Apostle Orson F. Whitney also spoke about spiritualism:

"Spiritualism is not altogether what some people imagine. Despite the frauds connected with it, it is a reality, and was recognized as such long before Sir Oliver Lodge and Sir A. Conan Doyle proclaimed their conversion thereto, thus lending to it the prestige of their illustrious names. But all realities are not righteous. Because there is a devil – an actual demon and his dupes – is no reason why we should associate with them, confide in them, or accept their evil communications."[4]

Elder James H. Moyle spoke about spiritualism in General Conference:

"Fifty years ago or more when I was a boy, and when spiritualism was being introduced, I heard the elders of the Church say that the time would come when all of the great truths of the gospel would in some way be more or less duplicated, as spiritualism was then attempting to duplicate one of the features of the truth revealed in our time. Later came a science of healing, by faith and a popular religion, its chief corner stone being healing by faith."[5]

The modern new age movement has many roots going back to Helena Blavatsky, a Russian occultist, spirit medium, and author who co-founded the Theosophical Society in 1875. Some of the others considered *founders* of the modern new age movement are: David Spangler, Barbara Marx Hubbard, Neale Donald Walsch, and Alice Bailey. Blavatsky taught that "it is Satan who is the God of our planet and the only God. Satan (or Lucifer) represents the Centrifugal Energy of the Universe"[6]. She wrote a book entitled *The Secret Doctrine: The Synthesis of Science, Religion, and Philosophy*. Part of the stated goal of this movement is to help the cause of a one world government and one world religion.

# # #

Recommended Resources:

- Book: *Search online for: Beware! The New Age Movement Is More Than Self-Indulgent Silliness: A Comprehensive Exposé of The New Age Movement*

- Video: *The New Age Agenda Explained.* YouTube, RockingMrE channel

BEWARE OF PRIDE

Some might wonder why the topic of pride would be included in a course on liberty? One of the fruits of pride is secret combinations. Pride results in a loss of liberty. It is only righteousness, repentance, and following God's Law that leads to freedom and liberty. Pride is therefore one of the greatest enemies of liberty.

From the talk *Beware of Pride* by Ezra Taft Benson:

"When pride has a hold on our hearts, we lose our independence of the world and deliver our freedoms to the bondage of men's judgment. The world shouts louder than the whisperings of the Holy Ghost. The reasoning of men overrides the revelations of God, and the proud let go of the iron rod.

"Pride is a sin that can readily be seen in others but is rarely admitted in ourselves. Most of us consider pride to be a sin of those on the top, such as the rich and the learned, looking down at the rest of us. There is, however, a far more common ailment among us—and that is pride from the bottom looking up. It is manifest in so many ways, such as faultfinding, gossiping, backbiting, murmuring, living beyond our means, envying, coveting, withholding gratitude and praise that might lift another, and being unforgiving and jealous.

"Disobedience is essentially a prideful power struggle against someone in authority over us. It can be a parent, a priesthood leader, a teacher, or ultimately God. A proud person hates the fact that someone is above him. He thinks this lowers his position.

"Selfishness is one of the more common faces of pride. "How everything affects me" is the center of all that matters—self-conceit, self-pity, worldly self-fulfillment, self-gratification, and self-seeking.

"Pride results in secret combinations which are built up to get power, gain, and glory of the world. This fruit of the sin of pride, namely secret combinations, brought down both the Jaredite and the Nephite civilizations and has been and will yet be the cause of the fall of many nations.

"Another face of pride is contention. Arguments, fights, unrighteous dominion, generation gaps, divorces, spouse abuse, riots, and disturbances all fall into this category of pride."[1]

In Ezra Taft Benson's message *The Price of Liberty: Eternal Vigilance*, he spoke of a political cycle very much similar to the pride cycle Latter-day Saints are familiar with, from reading the Book of Mormon:

"...Great nations do not usually fall by external aggression; they first erode and decay inwardly, so that, like rotten fruit, they fall of themselves. The history of nations shows that the cycle of the body politic slowly but surely undergoes change. It progresses — From bondage to spiritual faith — From spiritual faith to courage — From courage to freedom — From freedom to abundance — From abundance to selfishness — From selfishness to complacency — From complacency to apathy — From apathy to fear — From fear to dependency — From dependency to bondage."[2]

Quoting again from *Beware of Pride* by Ezra Taft Benson:

"Pride affects all of us at various times and in various degrees. Now you can see why the building in Lehi's dream that represents the pride of the world was large and spacious and great was the multitude that did enter into it. Pride is the universal sin, the great vice. Yes, pride is the universal sin, the great vice. The antidote for pride is humility—meekness, submissiveness. It is the broken heart and contrite spirit...

"My dear brethren and sisters, we must prepare to redeem Zion. It was essentially the sin of pride that kept us from establishing Zion in the days of the Prophet Joseph Smith. It was the same sin of pride that brought consecration to an end among the Nephites. Pride is the great stumbling block to Zion. I repeat: Pride is the great stumbling block to Zion."

# # #

Recommended Resources:

- Article: *Beware of Pride* by Ezra Taft Benson. Find at: latterdayconservative.com

- Video: *Beware of Pride* by Ezra Taft Benson. Find on YouTube

THE MAJESTY OF
GOD'S LAW

What's is God's Law? And what relation should exist between God's Law and Man's Law? These are excellent questions. In this lesson we will quote several excerpts from the book, *The Majesty of God's Law,* by W. Cleon Skousen. I highly recommend that you read the entire book for a better understanding of God's Law; how it was applied in ancient times, what America's Founding Fathers learned from studying the law of God as found in the Bible, and what is coming to America in preparing for the coming of the political Kingdom of God.

In a fireside on *Law and Becoming,* Elder D. Todd Christofferson said:

"Latter-day Saints would necessarily be included among those who believe in preexisting and universal natural law—or, as we might express it, law rooted in the preexisting justice and order of God. I firmly agree that insofar as humanly possible, man's laws and legal systems should be tied to God's laws and should reflect the same ultimate purpose: to foster our becoming all that we can become here and hereafter. People instinctively appreciate the value of law that has valid moral underpinnings because it is in their nature as spiritual beings and children of God—the ultimate moral Being. The light of Christ that we sometimes call conscience lights every person who comes into this world."[1]

Joseph Smith said the following about God's use of law:

"The first principles of man are self-existent with God. God himself, finding he was in the midst of spirits and glory, because he was more intelligent, saw proper to institute laws whereby the rest could have a privilege to advance like himself. The relationship we have with God places us in a situation to advance in knowledge. He has power to institute laws to instruct the weaker intelligences, that they may be exalted with Himself, so that they might have one glory upon another."[2]

Quoting from W. Cleon Skousen's *Majesty of God's Law*:

"Very often we hear people say, "Where did the Founding Fathers get so many of their great ideas?"

"Recently, Dr. Donald S. Lutz and Dr. Charles S. Hyneman made an extensive study to determine which books the Founders relied upon for the basic ideas that went into the formulation of the United

States Constitution. They reviewed an estimated 15,000 items, and closely perused the political content of 2,200 books, pamphlets, newspaper articles, and monographs which were published between 1760 and 1805. The most significant items were selected which amounted to 916 articles. These were carefully analyzed and numerically coded as to content as well as the references cited by the leaders of that era.

"It very quickly became apparent where the focus of interest was concentrated in the minds of the Founding Fathers. Of the thousands of citations quoted to support their ideas, 34% came from one source – the Bible. Most of these were from the book of Deuteronomy which is the Book of God's Law.

"Other citations were scattered over a broad spectrum of writings from historians, philosophers and political thinkers including Montesquieu, Blackstone, Locke, Coke, Cicero, and other intellectual luminaries from the so-called 'Enlightenment.' But the linchpin that united their thinking on every important principle was the Bible.

"Benjamin Franklin was largely self-taught which means he became his own tutor. The thoroughness of his studies persuaded him that the key to good government and happy living was centered in the Bible. He wrote his own creed and a devotional for private worship at the age of 22. At the age of 41 he wrote:

'As the scriptures are given for our reproof, instruction and warning, may we make a due use of this example, before it is too late.'

"To unite the American people, the Founders undertook to find those basic beliefs set forth in the Bible on which people of all religious faiths could agree. It turned out that Benjamin Franklin struck the most harmonious chord for everyone in his own personal creed. In a letter to Ezra Stiles, president of Yale University, the 81-year-old Franklin wrote:

'Here is my creed: I believe in one God, the Creator of the universe. That he governs it by his providence. That he ought to be worshiped. That the most acceptable service we render to him is in doing good to his other children. That the soul of man is immortal, and will be treated with justice in another life respecting its conduct in this. These I take to be the fundamental points in all sound religion.'

"A careful analysis of Franklin's creed reflects five points of fundamental religious belief which are either expressed or implied and these have been guideposts for Americans for over two centuries. Perhaps these could be summarized as follows:

1. There exists a Creator who made all things, and mankind should recognize and worship him.

2. The Creator has revealed a moral code of behavior for happy living which distinguishes right from wrong.

3. The Creator holds mankind responsible for the way they treat one another.

4. All mankind live beyond this life.

5. In the next life mankind are judged for their conduct in this one.

"All five of these tenets are abundantly evident throughout the writings of the Founding Fathers.

"Before closing this chapter, we should comment briefly on the long-range vision of the Founders concerning America. Their writings clearly demonstrate that these highly motivated leaders believed they were raised up by God to establish the United States as the first free people in modern times. They believed that their new commonwealth of freedom would eventually encompass the entire North American continent, and they held to this view in spite of the claims of England, Russia, France, and Spain to substantial parts of it.

"In fact, the American leaders were deeply disappointed when the four French colonies in Canada declined to accept the invitation extended to them in the Articles of Confederation to become an important part of the United States.

"Nevertheless, the Founders continued to express their complete confidence that their commonwealth would continue to expand, and many new states would be added to the Union until it extended from the Atlantic seaboard to the shores of the Pacific.

The Structure of God's Law

"Throughout his writings Moses continually refers to the Law of the Covenant or God's law as having three separate parts. Both the Lord and his prophet refer to these as follows:

1. The Commandments. This is the famous decalogue of ten commandments given to Moses in the presence of all of Israel at the foot of Mount Sinai and later inscribed on two stone tablets by the finger of God.

2. The Statutes. These are God's laws that John Adams called the "divine science" of good government for happy living and the complete formula for an ideal society. The Psalmist referred to these statutes as being "perfect ... right ... and pure."

3. The Judgments. These are the two kinds of judgments which God has held in reserve for the righteous who deserve "blessings" and the punishment for the wicked who deserve "cursings."

The Carnal Commandments Are Not Part

of God's Original Law

"It will be obvious as we go through God's law why we have not included any of the hated, tedious, boring ritual, diets, and litany of the Carnal Commandments in this study. As Paul explains, the law of Carnal Commandments was designed to teach the people the rhythm of obedience and hold the remnant of Israel together until Christ was born. Once this had transpired, the purpose of the Schoolmaster Law was fulfilled and its requirements repealed.

"Jesus verified that his life and ministry fulfilled the need for the Law of Carnal Commandments when he said:

'Think not that I am come to destroy the law ... but to fulfill.'

Judges must Be Righteous Men Acting in the Name of God

"Although the people were allowed to "take" or elect their own judges, they had to be brought to Moses for approval. These men had to be capable of wise and compassionate decisions. They had to govern the people of their particular group. In time of war, they had to be "captains." This selection process called for a very high caliber of men.

"Moses brought these leaders together to give them their instructions. He said:

'And I charged your judges at that time, saying, Hear the causes between your brethren, and judge righteously between every man and his brother, and the stranger that is with him.'

The Importance of Voluntary Obedience

"God's law is to be obeyed voluntarily rather than by compulsion. Therefore Moses read the entire law to his people and then we read:

'Moses came and called for the elders of the people, and laid before their faces all these words which the Lord commanded him. And all the people answered together, and said, All that the Lord hath spoken we will do. And Moses returned the words of the people unto the Lord.'

"When it says "Moses returned the words of the people unto the Lord," it simply means that they had heard the law, they understood the law, and they were willing to abide by it."[3]

Marion G. Romney taught about *The Perfect Law of Liberty* saying:

"I saw on a building the inscription 'Obedience to Law is Liberty.' With the proper interpretation of the word law, we have in this inscription a statement of ultimate truth. By inserting three words, it is made to read, 'Obedience to the law of Christ is liberty.' (See D&C 88:21.)

"This is not only a statement of the perfect law of liberty, but also a statement of the way to perfect liberty.

"In the eighth chapter of John is recorded a controversy between Jesus and the rulers of the Jews. They, of course, rejected him. But some who heard believed, and to them he said, "If ye continue in my word, then are ye my disciples indeed;

'And ye shall know the truth, and the truth shall make you free.' (John 8:31–32.)

"Freedom thus obtained — that is, by obedience to the law of Christ — is freedom of the soul, the highest form of liberty. And the most glorious thing about it is that it is within the reach of every one of us, regardless of what people about us, or even nations, do. All we have to do is learn the law of Christ and obey it. To learn it and obey it is the primary purpose of every soul's mortal life.

In closing, quoting again from *The Majesty of God's Law*:

The Challenge for Today

"America can be 'the Peacemaker of the World.' She can help other nations discover the formula for freedom and prosperity. But there is an important prerequisite: Americans must first rediscover that formula for themselves, as it is embodied in the principles found in the Constitution.

"It is helpful to remember that the Constitution is not a stale, dead document. Rather, it is a vital, living blueprint for the success of the United States as a nation and its citizens as individuals.

"A quick comparison between the constitutional principles and our practices today will show where we have gone astray. And the remedy is simple: return to the basic principles of the Founders' formula.

"Of course, the first step to improvement and reform is education. The next step is action. The principles of the Constitution were not meant only to be studied, but to be restored and put into full operation."[4]

# # #

Recommended Resources:

- Book: *The Majesty of God's Law: It's coming to America* by W. Cleon Skousen. Available at: amazon.com

- Article/Audio: *Socialism and the United* Order by Marion G. Romney. Find at: latterdayconservative.com

- Article: *The United Order vs. Communism* by J. Reuben Clark, Jr.. Find at: latterdayconservative.com

BECOMING ZION

It seems only appropriate when discussing Zion to share what the prophet Joseph Smith said about it:

"We ought to have the building up of Zion as our greatest object.

"Speaking of the Land of Zion that it consists of all North & South America but that any place where the Saints gather is Zion which every righteous man will build up for a place of safety for his children...

"Zion and Jerusalem and must both be built up before the coming of Christ."[1]

Also, from *Teachings of the Prophet Joseph Smith*:

"Zion ... is a place of righteousness, and all who build thereon are to worship the true and living God, and all believe in one doctrine, even the doctrine of our Lord and Savior Jesus Christ."

Elder D. Todd Christofferson said:

"Zion is both a place and a people.

"The Lord called Enoch's people Zion 'because they were of one heart and one mind, and dwelt in righteousness; and there was no poor among them' (Moses 7:18). Elsewhere He said, 'For this is Zion—the pure in heart' (D&C 97:21).

"Under the direction of the Prophet Joseph Smith, early members of the Church attempted to establish the center place of Zion in Missouri, but they did not qualify to build the holy city. The Lord explained one of the reasons for their failure:

'They have not learned to be obedient to the things which I required at their hands, but are full of all manner of evil, and do not impart of their substance, as becometh saints, to the poor and afflicted among them;

'And are not united according to the union required by the law of the celestial kingdom" (D&C 105:3–4).

'There were jarrings, and contentions, and envyings, and strifes, and lustful and covetous desires among them; therefore by these things they polluted their inheritances' (D&C 101:6)."4

Hugh Nibley wrote a lot about this topic in his book *Approaching Zion*:

"Modern revelation has some interesting things to say about idlers: 'Let every man be diligent in all things. And the idler shall not have place in the church' (D&C 75:29). We are all to work in the kingdom and for the kingdom. 'And the inhabitants of Zion also shall remember their labors, inasmuch as they are appointed to labor,...for the idler shall be had in remembrance before the Lord' (D&C 68:30).

"Note that it is not the withholding of lunch but the observant eye of the Lord that admonishes the idler. This refers to all of us as laborers in Zion, and 'the laborer in Zion shall labor for Zion; for if they labor for money they shall perish' (2 Nephi 26:31). That is the theme here: 'Now, I, the Lord, am not well pleased with the inhabitants of Zion, for there are idlers among them;... they also seek not earnestly the riches of eternity, but their eyes are full of greediness' (D&C 68:31).

"An idler in the Lord's book is one who is not working for the building up of the kingdom of God on earth and the establishment of Zion, no matter how hard he may be working to satisfy his own greed."4

Also from *Approaching Zion*:

"There is no third way: 'Those who believe and obey the Gospel of the Son of God forsake all for its interests, belong to the kingdom of God, and all the rest belong to the other kingdom.'

"And so we have Zion and Babylon, and never the twain shall meet. That is, they wouldn't if we did not take human nature into account, for how many humans have ever succeeded in renouncing the world completely? The separation of the Saints from the world was, in most cases, not a matter of choice—it was forced on them; God is constantly driving wedges between the Church and the world, or in Brigham Young's vivid terms, there are always cats coming out of the bag to put us at odds with the world, whether we want it that way or not.

'The brethren and sisters came across the plains because they could not stay; that is the secret of the movement. Do you think we came here of our own choice? No; we would have stayed in those rich valleys and prairies back yonder.'

"When the first revelation was given to prepare for Zion by the gathering of Israel,

'when the people came to Jackson county, ... they were as far from believing and obeying that revelation as the east is from the west. And so we have got to continue to labor, fight, toil, counsel, exercise faith, ask God over and over, and have been praying for thirty odd years for that which we might have received and accomplished in one year.'

"That complete break between the Saints and the world that must precede the coming of Zion has not yet taken place.

'They have not learned 'a' concerning Zion; and we have been traveling now forty-two years, and have we learned our a, b, c's? ... I will say, scarcely. Have we seen it as a people? How long shall we travel, ... how long shall God wait for us to sanctify ourselves and become one in the Lord, in our actions and in our ways for the building up of the kingdom of God, that he can bless us?'

'How long, Latter-day Saints, before you will believe the Gospel as it is? The Lord has declared it to be his will that his people will enter into covenant, even as Enoch and his people did, which of necessity, must be before we shall have the privilege of building the Center Stake of Zion.'

"This was one of the last public addresses of the prophet Brigham, and the people were still not ready to go all the way. They still wanted to mix Babylon and Zion; or, as he put it, 'Some of the Latter-day Saints had an idea that they could take the follies of the world in one hand and the Savior in the other, and expect to get into the presence of the Lord Jesus.' Such heaping up gold and silver would prove their destruction.

"Again and again the Lord had to rebuke even Joseph Smith for little concessions to the world:

'You have feared man and have not relied on me for strength as you ought' (D&C 30:1).

'Your mind has been on the things of the earth more than on the things of me, ... and you ... have been persuaded by those whom I have not commanded; ... you shall ever open your mouth in my cause, not fearing what man can do, for I am with you' (D&C 30:2, 11).

'How oft you have transgressed the commandments and the laws of God, and have gone on in the persuasions of men. For behold you should not have feared man more than God' (D&C 3:6-7)."

Ezra Taft Benson, in a talk entitled *A Witness and a Warning*, said:

"Men who are wise, good, and honest, who will uphold the Constitution of the United States in the tradition of the Founding Fathers, must be sought for diligently. This is our hope to restore government to its rightful role. I fully believe that we can turn things around in America if we have the determination, the morality, the patriotism, and the spirituality to do so...

"...I further witness that this land — the Americas — must be protected, its Constitution upheld, for this is a land foreordained to be the Zion of our God. He expects us as members of the Church and bearers of His priesthood to do all we can to preserve our liberty."5

In his book *The Government of God*, John Taylor wrote about the coming Kingdom of God and Zion:

"How will the kingdom of God be established? We have already shown very clearly, that none of the means which are now used among men are commensurate with the object designed, and that all the combined wisdom of man must, and will fail, in the accomplishment of this object; that the present forms of political and religious rule cannot effect it; that philosophy is quite as impotent; and that as these have all failed for ages, as a natural consequence they must continue to fail. We have portrayed the world broken, corrupted, fallen, degraded and ruined; and shown that nothing but a world's God can put it right.

"The question is, what course will God take for the accomplishment of this thing? and as this is a matter that requires more than human reason, and as we are left entirely to Revelation, either past, present, or to come, it is to this only that we can apply. We will enquire, therefore, what the Scriptures say on this subject. It is called the kingdom of God, or the kingdom of heaven. If, therefore, it is the kingdom of heaven, it must receive its laws, organization, and government, from heaven; for if they were earthly, then would they be like those on the earth. The kingdom of heaven must therefore be the government, and laws of heaven, on the earth. If the government and laws of heaven are known and observed on the earth, they must be communicated, or revealed from the heavens to the earth. These things are plain and evident, if we are to have any kingdom of heaven, for it is very clear, that if it is not God's rule, it cannot be his government, and it is as evident that if it is not revealed from heaven it cannot be the kingdom of heaven.

"...For 'when the Lord shall build up Zion, he shall appear in his glory,' and not before. But if Zion is never built up, the Lord never will come, for he must have a people, and a place to come to. The prophets hailed this day with pleasure, as the ushering in of those glorious times, which were to follow. Micah says, 'But in the last days it shall come to pass, that the mountain of the house of the Lord shall be established in the top of the mountains, and it shall be exalted above the hills; and people shall flow unto it. And many nations shall come, and say, Come, and let us go up to the mountain of the Lord, and to the house of the God of Jacob; and he will teach us of his ways, and we will walk in his paths; for the law shall go forth of Zion, and the word of the Lord from Jerusalem.'"[6]

# # #

Recommended Resources:

- Book: *Approaching Zion* by Hugh Nibley. Available at: amazon.com or read online

- Article: *What We Might Expect in the Next Twenty-Five*

Years by W. Cleon Skousen. Find at: latterdayconservative.com

- Book: *The Government of God* by John Taylor. Available to read online

FINAL THOUGHTS

Now that I know, WHAT SHOULD I DO?

It's the question I hear being asked over and over again. "Now what? You've taught all these great principles, you've told me the world is going to pieces, now I want to know what to do about it."

It's an important question for sure, and many are not satisfied with the answer to that question. They are not satisfied because people have been *doing* these things for years with seemingly no results. Maybe the problem is that they aren't realizing what the results are, or are hoping for certain results in vain. You might be doing all the right things yet nothing around you is changing, the world is getting more and more wicked, governments are becoming more and more corrupt. Perhaps we won't fix the world's problems but if sharing the truth is of value to just one individual then it's worth it to me. What if the important thing is that this information causes people to live their own lives in accordance with correct principles and adjust the way they think and view the world. This work is about saving souls and standing up for truth and right. It starts with you, and from there to your family, and friends, and neighbors, and so on.

The Lord wins in the end

"This is still God's world. The forces of evil, working through some mortals, have made a mess of a good part of it. But it is still God's world. In due time, when each of us has had a chance to prove ourselves – including whether or not we are going to stand up for freedom – God will interject himself, and the final and eternal victory shall be for free agency. And then shall those complacent people on the sidelines, and those who took the wrong but temporarily popular course, lament their decisions. To the patriots I say this: Take that long eternal look. Stand up for freedom, no matter what the cost. Stand up and be counted. It can help to save your soul – and maybe your country. (Ezra Taft Benson, *Teachings of Ezra Taft Benson*)

A great man and friend of freedom, W. Cleon Skousen, often said in response to those who would ask him why he was always so optimistic despite the apparent wickedness in the world, "We have read the last chapter, we know who wins in the end. In the end, the Lord prevails!"

Not always wise to expose evil

I think it's always a good idea to consider the best strategy and tactic for each situation, and seek inspiration as well. Sometimes in order to influence people you may have to avoid talking about certain subjects. There may even be principles that you understand that you must keep to yourself or certain things you might discuss in private but not in public.

We have been told to "waste and wear out our lives in bringing to light all the hidden things of darkness, wherein we know them; and they are truly manifest from heaven — these should then be attended to with great earnestness." (D&C 122:13.)

Contrast that statement with what Joseph Smith taught:

"It is not always wise to relate all the truth. Even Jesus, the Son of God, had to refrain from doing so, and had to restrain His feelings many times for the safety of Himself and His followers, and had to conceal the righteous purposes of His heart in relation to many things pertaining to His Father's kingdom. When still a boy He had all the intelligence necessary to enable Him to rule and govern the kingdom of the Jews, and could reason with the wisest and most profound doctors of law and divinity, and make their theories and practice to appear like folly compared with the wisdom He possessed; but He was a boy only, and lacked physical strength even to defend His own person; and was subject to cold, to hunger and to death. So it is with the Church of Jesus Christ of Latter-day Saints; we have the revelation of Jesus, and the knowledge within us is sufficient to organize a righteous government upon the earth, and to give universal peace to all mankind, if they would receive it, but we lack the physical strength, as did our Savior when a child, to defend our principles, and we have a necessity to be afflicted, persecuted and smitten, and to bear it patiently until Jacob is of age, then he will take care of himself." (Joseph Smith, *Teachings of the Prophet Joseph Smith.*)

It's important, especially from a strategical perspective, to consider the meaning of both of those statements in regards to how we choose to act on our knowledge of the principles of liberty, the Gospel, secret combinations, etc.

Do you know why many are called but few are chosen?

According to David O. McKay, Section 121 of the *Doctrine and Covenants* is "the greatest revelation that God has ever given to man." (BYU Speeches of the year, Alvin R. Dyer, March 20, 1963.)

In that revelation we read: "Amen to the priesthood or the authority of that man" who uses "control or dominion or compulsion upon the souls of the children of men, in any degree of unrighteousness." This does not just apply to priesthood holders but anyone in a position of "authority" (such as in government).

H. Verlan Andersen, author of *Many Are Called But Few Are Chosen* (a book that I highly recommend), wrote about this topic at length. I will quote from an article he wrote entitled *Do You Know Why Many Are Called But Few Are Chosen?*:

"Government has an exclusive monopoly on the use of force in that it is the only organization legally authorized to compel people against their will. Unless we desire to use force, we do not use government. If we want only voluntary cooperation, we use a church, a club, a lodge, or some other non-compulsory organization. The only ones who join such groups are those who want to. The only ones who pay dues and obey the rules are those who do so of their own free will and choice. It is only when we want to compel those people to join, pay dues, and obey the rules who would not do so unless threatened with physical violence, that we resort to the use of government and law.

"Assuming that God holds us accountable for any force used by our government of which we approve, is it reasonable to believe that 'almost all men' might be losing their priesthood by abusing this power which God has placed in our hands?

"There are literally thousands of laws on both the state and federal level for the citizen to pass judgment on. It seems very likely that 'almost all' of us would support some laws which would constitute unrighteous dominion unless we were very careful. This seems especially true in view of the fact that 'it is the nature and disposition of almost all men' to abuse any power given them.

"Is not the Lord expecting too much in requiring us to distinguish with precision between those laws which preserve freedom and those which destroy it?

"It is no more difficult to distinguish between good and bad 'group action' than to distinguish between good and bad individual action because the test is the same in both cases. D&C 134:4-5 tell us that the civil magistrate should never violate freedom of conscience. This is an application of the *Golden Rule* which we use to judge individual action. It provides, in effect, that we should never favor a law which would take from another any freedom which we would desire for ourselves. Since every person loves his freedom and knows exactly what will injure or destroy it, this knowledge enables him to know exactly what he should not do to his neighbor either through government or otherwise. In applying the *Golden Rule* test we might ask ourselves such questions as these:

"1. Remembering that I am individually accountable for the force used under any law which I favor, would it violate my conscience to enact this law myself and then personally punish my neighbors if they disobeyed it?

"2. If I had violated this law, would my conscience tell me I had done evil?

"3. Remembering that every law either compels or restrains a person against his will, I should place myself in the position of the one against whom the law will be enforced and ask if I would consider it fair to have my own freedom of action restrained in the manner required by the law.

"Why would the Lord deprive a man of his priesthood because of false political beliefs and practices?

"Because when we abandon the principles of freedom contained in the Constitution, we reject Christ's plan to preserve freedom (D&C 101:77, 78), and substitute in place thereof Satan's plan to destroy freedom. It will be recalled that in the pre-earth life, Satan proposed a plan of compulsion to destroy the agency of man on this earth. The Lord divided us up on the basis of whether we accepted or rejected that plan. However since almost all of us who rejected that plan are still inclined to exercise unrighteous dominion when given the opportunity, it was necessary that Satan be allowed to continue to tempt us to accept it here in order that we might completely overcome this weakness.

"D&C Sec. 121 tells us that if, at the end of this life, we are still inclined to use Satan's methods, the Lord will not be able to entrust us with His Priesthood power in the hereafter."

The truth really does make us free.

CITATIONS

Chapter 1
The War in Heaven on Earth Today

1. Ezra Taft Benson, *Stand Up for Freedom*. Assembly Hall, Temple Square, Feb 1966.
2. David O. McKay, *Two Contending Forces*. May 18, 1960.
3. Ezra Taft Benson, *The Constitution a Heavenly Banner*. Sep 16, 1986.
4. Marion G. Romney. General Conference, April 1966.
5. John Taylor. General Conference, April 1882.
6. L. Tom Perry, *Truth and Liberty*. BYU, Sep 1987.
7. Joseph F. Smith. General Conference, April 1946.
8. Joseph Fielding Smith, *Doctrines of Salvation, Vol. 3*, pp.314-315.
9. Ezra Taft Benson, *Secret Combinations*. General Conference, Oct 1961.
10. Ezra Taft Benson, *Civic Standards for the Faithful Saints*. General Conference, Apr 1972.
11. Ezra Taft Benson, *Not Commanded in All Things*. General Conference, Apr 1965.
12. Ezra Taft Benson, *Our Immediate Responsibility*. BYU Devotional, Oct 25, 1966.
13. Shirley D. Christensen, *"I, the Lord God, Make You Free"*. Ensign, Feb 2006.
14. Gordon B. Hinckley, The War We Are Winning. Ensign, June 2007.
15. James E. Faust, *The Forces That Will Save Us*. Ensign, Jan 2007.
16. Ezra Taft Benson, General Conference, Sep 1961.

Chapter 2
Life, Liberty and the Pursuit of Happiness

1. Ezra Taft Benson, *The Proper Role of Government*. 1968.
2. David O. McKay, *Free Agency, A Divine Gift*. Improvement Era, May 1950, 366.
3. Russell M. Nelson, *Now Is the Time to Prepare*. Ensign, May 2005, 16.

Chapter 3
The Proper Role of Government

1. H. Verlan Andersen, *Thoughts on Agency. Life and Teachings*, 2007.
2. Frédéric Bastiat, *The Law*. 1850.
3. Ezra Taft Benson, *The Proper Role of Government*. 1968.

Chapter 4
Overview of America

1. Ezra Taft Benson, *America, A Choice Land*. General Conference, Apr 1962.
2. Ezra Taft Benson. *Title of Liberty* 176; from an address given at Los Angeles, CA, Dec 11, 1961.
3. Ezra Taft Benson, *Teachings of Ezra Taft Benson* 602.
4. W. Cleon Skousen, *100 Things Destroying America*. 1982.
5. W. Cleon Skousen, *100 Things Destroying America*. 1982.
6. Ezra Taft Benson, America at the Crossroads. New Era, July 1978, 36.

Chapter 5
The Constitution: A Heavenly Banner

1. Joseph Smith, *History of the Church* 6:198.
2. Joseph Smith, *Teachings of the Prophet Joseph Smith* 147-48.
3. Gordon B. Hinckley, *Keep Faith with America*. May 6, 1999.
4. Heber J. Grant, *Admonition and Blessing*, 694-95.
5. Ezra Taft Benson, *The Constitution: A Heavenly Banner*. September 16, 1986.

Chapter 6
Freedom and Free Enterprise

1. Ayn Rand, *Capitalism: The Unknown Ideal.* 1966.
2. Howard W. Hunter, The Law of the Harvest. BYU Devotional, Mar 8, 1966.
3. Ezra Taft Benson, *Freedom and Free Enterprise.* 1977.

Chapter 7
War and Foreign Policy

1. Spencer W. Kimball, *The False Gods We Worship.* First Presidency Message, June 1976.
2. W. Cleon Skousen, *The War Powers and the Remaining Enumerated Powers. The Making of America*, Chapter 18.
3. Thomas Jefferson, quoted in *The Making of America*, Chapter 18, W. Cleon Skousen.
4. Benjamin Franklin, quoted in *The Making of America*, Chapter 18, W. Cleon Skousen.
5. James Madison, quoted in *The Making of America*, Chapter 18, W. Cleon Skousen.
6. George Washington, *Farewell Address.* 1796.
7. Ezra Taft Benson, *United States Foreign Policy.* Farm Bureau Banquet in Preston, Idaho, June 21, 1968.

Chapter 8
The Hidden Things of Darkness: Political Secret Combinations

1. Ezra Taft Benson, *Civic Standards for the Faithful Saints.* Ensign, July 1972, 59.
2. John Taylor, *Deseret News*, April 13, 1886.
3. David O. McKay, *Gospel Ideals*, p. 306.
4. Ezra Taft Benson. General Conference, Oct 1961.
5. Ezra Taft Benson, *I Testify.* General Conference, Oct 1988.
6. Abe Day, *The 11th Commandment of the Book of Mormon.* Published on mormonchronicle.com, 2009.

Chapter 9

Opposition in All Things: Spiritual Secret Combinations

1. Joseph F. Smith, *Gospel Doctrine*, p.503.
2. James E. Talmage, *Articles of Faith*, p.211.
3. James E. Talmage, *Articles of Faith*, p.211.
4. Orson F. Whitney, *Saturday Night Thoughts – Do The Dead Return?*. Deseret News, 1921.
5. James H. Moyle. General Conference, Oct 1929.
6. Helena Blavatsky, *The Secret Doctrine*, Vol. 2, p.234. 1888.

Chapter 10
Beware of Pride

1. Ezra Taft Benson, *Beware of Pride*. General Conference, Apr 1989.
2. Ezra Taft Benson, *The Price of Liberty: Eternal Vigilance. This Nation Shall Endure*, 1977.

Chapter 11
The Majesty of God's Law

1. D. Todd Christofferson, *Law and Becoming*. Fireside presented to the J. Reuben Clark Law Society, Feb 4, 2011.
2. Joseph Smith, *The King Follett Sermon*. General Conference, April 7, 1844.
3. W. Cleon Skousen, *The Majesty of God's Law*. 1996.
4. Marion G. Romney, *The Perfect Law of Liberty*. Ensign, Nov 1981, 43.
5. W. Cleon Skousen, *The Majesty of God's Law*. 1996.

Chapter 12
Becoming Zion

1. Joseph Smith, July 19, 1840. *Words of Joseph Smith*, 1980.
2. Joseph Smith. *Teachings of the Prophet Joseph Smith*, compiled by Joseph Fielding Smith. 1976.
3. D. Todd Christofferson, *Come to Zion*. Gen. Conf., Oct 2008.
4. Hugh Nibley, *Approaching Zion*. 1989.
5. Ezra Taft Benson, *A Witness and a Warning*. Ensign, Nov. 1979.
6. John Taylor. *The Government of God*, Chapter XI, 1852.

ABOUT THE AUTHOR

This book was written and compiled by Brian Mecham, founder of the *Ezra Taft Benson Society* and creator of latterdayconservative.com - a website that provides educational resources that promote the principles of Liberty based on the Gospel of Jesus Christ.

From knowledge comes strength, and from strength comes the power to preserve freedom both at home and abroad... knowledge is strength to a free people. (Ezra Taft Benson)

Ye shall know the truth and the truth shall set you free. (John 8:32)

Made in the USA
San Bernardino, CA
18 January 2020